PRAISE FOR SUSAN'S W

"Since the murder of her niece Maggie, Susan has been an agent of positive change for victims and offenders alike, strengthening those hurt and converting those who harm. Words can hurt but also transform, and Susan's work in the Thriver Zone shows you how."

—CHARLENE SMITH, A SOUTH AFRICAN MULTI-AWARD-WINNING JOURNALIST, AN AUTHORIZED BIOGRAPHER OF NELSON MANDELA, AUTHOR OF PROUD OF ME: SPEAKING OUT AGAINST SEXUAL VIOLENCE AND HIV

"Susan's unique experience working with both victims and offenders alike and her strength-based approach to focusing on the goal of thriving makes her books an exceptional tool for survivors of abuse as well as the professionals working with them so they can move forward into a more positive part of their lives."

—LINDA MCMURRAY LCSW, DOMESTIC VIOLENCE COUNSELOR

"Susan's work and trainings are inspirational and motivational. Native women tell me that by focusing them on the goal of not being stuck in abuse, Susan gives them a choice to thrive, not just survive their experiences. They gain a sense of self-worth that has made a difference in their lives. We are truly blessed to have met Susan and been able to work with her."

—SANDRA TOSCANO, TRIBAL DOMESTIC VIOLENCE AND SEXUAL ASSAULT ADVOCATE

PRAISE FOR SUSAN FROM WOMEN IN HER WORKSHOPS

"I am so grateful that my path crossed with Susan Omilian's fifteen years ago. She and the women in the Thriver Community she has created helped me grow, get out of a dark place and raise my self-esteem. I have learned to love myself more and connect with the Happy Person Inside every day. Today I am happy and healthy. I am living well! I am a thriver!"

—ANNA

"Susan has helped me see that I'm worth it! I am living well – successfully employed, strong single parent and active community volunteer. I can think big and dream – focusing on my short- and long-term goals."

—DARLENE

"Susan is such an inspiration! Her work continues to help women to find their true selves. I will be forever grateful for her being in my life and showing me that I could do this – live the life of a thriver after abuse!"

—DONNA

"Because of Susan I believe I have a chance to live and thrive after abuse. She has helped me get out of a dark room and see the light."
—Gordana

"The greatest gift I have received being part of Susan's Thriver Community is encouragement, energy and enthusiasm to move forward with my life. I have grown personally and understand my heart better so that I can focus on my goals and dream a better future."
—Joal

"Susan has helped me look at the positive aspects of my life instead of the negative – the domestic violence I have experienced. I know now it is okay for me to want a better life for myself and for my children. I can dream and hope for my future and find my own destiny."
—Kathy

"Susan's workshops have made me feel special and given me inspiration. In Susan's Thriver Community, I can share with other women like me and work on myself. Living well after abuse means that I can find inner peace."
—Lisa R.

"Susan has been a godsend to me! Today I am a thriver, moving forward to continue my education and get a great job so that I can have a good, peaceful and productive life."
—Lisa S.

"Susan's work helped me to focus on the future. I have been able to define who I am, break out to freedom and pursue creative passions. I have enjoyed the friendship of the women I have met in the Thriver Community who have walked the same journey as mine."
—Pamela

"Susan's workshops have helped me come alive and know that I am somebody. Susan's Thriver Community has given me support, love and care. I'm doing things now I never would have done before due to low self-esteem."
—Vonda

"The greatest gift I have received as part of Susan's Thriver Community is how to stay positive and that I have a choice to keep pushing forward."
—Yvonne

Living in the Thriver Zone

A Celebration of Living Well as the Best Revenge

Susan M. Omilian JD

*Reclaiming the Lives of Women
Who Have Been Abused*

Butterfly Bliss Productions LLC
West Hartford, CT

Living in the Thriver Zone: A Celebration of Living Well as the Best Revenge

Copyright © 2020 by Susan M. Omilian

All rights reserved. No part of this book may be reproduced or transmitted in any form or by any means, electronic or mechanical, including photocopying, recording, or by an information storage and retrieval system — except by a reviewer who may quote brief passages in a review to be printed in a magazine, newspaper or on the Web — without permission in writing from the publisher. This book is available at quantity discounts for bulk purchase. For information, contact the publisher.

Butterfly Bliss Productions LLC
P.O. Box 330482, West Hartford, CT 06133
ButterflyBlissProductions.com
ThriverZone.com
SusanOmilian.com

ISBN # 978-0-9842509-7-4 printed book
ISBN # 978-0-9842509-6-7 e-book

Worksheets referenced in the text can be downloaded at "Resources" on *ThriverZone.com*.

Author photo by Cynthia Lang Photography
Maggie's photo by Joe Sherman | *PhotographicArtistry.net*
Front cover & interior design concept by Donna Gentile Creative | *DonnaGentileCreative.com*
Cover & interior production by Anita Jones, Another Jones Graphics | *AnotherJones.com*

A portion of the proceeds of this book will be donated to services for women and children who have experienced abuse and violence.

This book is available at quantity discounts for bulk purchase. For information, contact the publisher.

Publisher's Cataloging-In-Publication Data
(Prepared by The Donohue Group, Inc.)

Names: Omilian, Susan M., author.
Title: Living in the Thriver Zone : a celebration of living well as the best revenge / Susan M. Omilian JD.
Description: West Hartford, CT : Butterfly Bliss Productions LLC, [2020] | Series: [The Thriver Zone series] ; [3] | "Reclaiming the lives of women who have been abused." | Includes bibliographical references.
Identifiers: ISBN 9780984250974 (print) | ISBN 9780984250967 (ebook)
Subjects: LCSH: Abused women--Psychology. | Self-actualization (Psychology) in women. | Control (Psychology) | Happiness. | Quality of life.
Classification: LCC HV6626 .O452 2020 (print) | LCC HV6626 (ebook) | DDC 362.8292--dc23

Printed in the United States of America

DEDICATION

Dedicated to my niece Maggie (1980 – 1999)

**...and all the women inspired by her story
whose lives have been made better.**

I also dedicated this book to my niece,
Lindsey and her daughter, my grandniece Josie.

They are the future of women in our family
and the holders of the hope that we can create a world
where women are truly treated as equals
and with love and respect.

*The truest measure of our lives is not what we have experienced,
but what we have made of our experiences.*

~ Susan M. Omilian ~

ACKNOWLEDGMENTS

For all the women, survivors of abuse, who I have met and worked with for almost four decades, I admire your courage, persistence and refusal to let what has happened to you define who you are! I have learned from you what it truly means to live in the Thriver Zone.

Thanks to all for blessing my life with your heartfelt stories. Special thanks to Adrienne, Cathryn, Jenny, Pamela, Sophia, Tawanda and Tennille, whose extended, inspiring Thriver Success Stories appear in this book. I celebrate your resilience, your strength and your determination to move forward with your lives after abuse. You are living well!

Thanks to Anita Jones, an amazing book designer, Claudia Volkman for her keen eye in editing this book, and Sharon Castlen for her support, guidance and remarkable vision in marketing this book.

Most of all, thanks to all of you who have let me share your journey as you have shared mine and discover the life we were destined to live, the work that we were born to do.

Living well is our best revenge!

ABOUT THE AUTHOR

Susan Omilian is an attorney, award-winning author, and motivational speaker who has worked extensively as an advocate to end violence against women for the past forty years. In the 1970s, she founded a rape crisis center and represented battered women in divorce proceedings in the early 1980s. She also litigated sex discrimination cases including helping to articulate the legal concept that made sexual harassment illegal in the 1990s.

She is a published author of several books on sex discrimination law as well as articles for newspapers and journals, including *The Voice: The Journal of the Battered Women's Movement* published by the National Coalition Against Domestic Violence (NCADV). Susan holds a law degree from Wayne State University in Detroit and a bachelor of arts degree in journalism from the University of Michigan. She is licensed to practice law in both Connecticut and Michigan.

With the death of her nineteen-year-old niece Maggie, who was shot and killed in October 1999 by her ex-boyfriend, Susan's work on behalf of women became more personal and immediate. She vowed to help other women move on after abuse and create a new life for themselves and their children as Maggie could not.

Susan's other books in *The Thriver Zone Series*™ include *Entering the Thriver Zone: A Seven-Step Guide to Thriving After Abuse,* published in 2016 and *Staying in the Thriver Zone: A Road Map to Manifesting a Life of Power and Purpose* in 2018. Susan has also written two novels in her *The Best Revenge Series*™ inspired by the true event of the murder of her niece Maggie in 1999. The first is *Awaken: The Awakening of the Human Spirit on a Healing Journey* published in 2017; the second, *Emerge: The Opening of the Human Heart to the Power of Love,* was published in 2019.

SUSAN'S PERSONAL MISSION STATEMENT

"I am a woman of power whose mission in life is to be a catalyst for change for victims of violence against women. Today I celebrate my life by building a community of strong, independent, productive women who have survived abuse and are thriving in well-being, love, and joy."

ABOUT THE SPEAKER

Susan Omilian is an experienced, inspirational speaker with a dramatic story and a unique motivational model to share. She has helped hundreds of women reclaim their lives after abuse and take the journey from victim to survivor to "thriver!"

As the award-winning originator and facilitator since 2001 of My Avenging Angel Workshops™ based on the idea that "living well is the best revenge," Susan has developed a seven-step process to thriving after abuse. It has been described as "life-changing" and as "a component for women recovering from abuse that has been virtually overlooked." Susan delivers her message of hope and possibility for women with passion and enthusiasm fueled by her own personal tragedy—her niece Maggie's violent death. It is her firm belief that women who take the journey to thriving are less likely to return to an abusive relationship or suffer the long-term physical and psychological consequences of the abuse they have experienced.

With simple, invigorating writing exercises and inspirational success stories, Susan's books in *The Thriver Zone Series*™ include *Entering the Thriver Zone: A Seven-Step Guide to Thriving After Abuse, Staying in the Thriver Zone: A Road Map to Manifest a Life of Power and Purpose* and *Living in the Thriver Zone: A Celebration of Living Well as the Best Revenge.* These books set forth the motivational guidance she has successfully used with women over the last twenty years. Susan envisions that millions of women who have faced violence and abuse as well as their families, friends, counselors, therapists, and healthcare providers will find all her books in The *Thriver Zone Series*™ an invaluable guide to taking the life-changing journey from victim to survivor to thriver!

Susan is a recognized, articulate national expert on the process of recovery after violence and abuse. She has been invited to speak throughout the country by victim rights organizations such as National Organization of Victim Assistance (NOVA), before service providers and clinicians as well as to students and faculty on college campuses. She has also been a keynote speaker at domestic violence and sexual assault awareness events and a featured presenter at national meetings and international conferences sponsored by the Institute on Violence, Abuse and Trauma (IVAT).

Susan also regularly speaks to diverse audiences, including a men's prison in Massachusetts and a Pennsylvania women's prison, where her books and materials have been used with male and female inmates to help them to break the cycle of abuse and trauma in their lives. Her books have been purchased throughout the United States and appear in various countries including the Netherlands, New Zealand, Canada, South Africa, and American Samoa. Susan works with Indian tribes in California who, like others interested in her materials, have purchased multiple copies of her books and used them with individuals and groups in clinical and therapeutic settings as well as in victim assistance programs.

Susan's company, Butterfly Bliss Productions LLC, which publishes her non-fiction books and novels, is also developing an imprint, *Thriver Spirit Press,* to publish books and stories that epitomize the healing and inspirational energy of moving beyond struggle and abuse.

For more information about Susan's transformational work
or to arrange for her to speak at a meeting or event,
please visit *ThriverZone.com.*

CONTENTS

PAGE

About the Author ii
About the Speaker iii
Note from the Author — Living Well Is Our Best Revenge 1
How to Use This Book 2
Getting Started – Living Your Best Life as a Thriver............................... 3

Part One	Take the Journey 17	
	EXERCISE: Call to Adventure – A Thriver Hero's Journey	
Part Two	Be a Super Hero Thriver 33	
	EXERCISE: I am a Super Hero Thriver!	
Part Three	Find Tools for Your Journey 45	
	EXERCISE: Where Are You on Your Journey? Survey for Journey to Thriving	
	TOOL: *The Seven Steps to Thriving After Abuse*	
	TOOL: *A Road Map to Manifest a Life of Power and Purpose*	
	EXERCISE: Manifesting: A Fairy Tale	
Part Four	Thriver Success Stories 73	
	Meet the Super Hero Thrivers	
	Adrienne..93	
	Cathryn.. 100	
	Jenny.. 116	
	Pamela.. 131	
	Sophia 137	
	Tawanda... 144	
	Tennille... 152	
Part Five	Living in the Thriver Zone Toolbox 163	
	QUIZ: Are You Living in the Thriver Zone? 168	
Resources	 173	
	Outline of the My Avenging Angel Workshops™ Program	
	Speaker/Trainer Packet for Susan Omilian, Thriver Zone	
	Resources for Crisis Intervention, Domestic Violence, Sexual Assault	
	Books, Movies and Music to Accompany You on Your Journey	

*Then, living well is not
only the best revenge;
it is, in fact, the song of our souls and
the fulfillment of all of our dreams.*

– Susan M. Omilian JD

NOTE FROM THE AUTHOR – LIVING WELL IS OUR BEST REVENGE

On October 18, 1999, Maggie, my brother's nineteen-year-old stepdaughter, was murdered on a college campus by her ex-boyfriend, who then killed himself.

Shock, guilt and a cry for revenge welled up inside me, but what was I to do? I couldn't save Maggie. No one had seen the danger she was in after she ended the relationship, not even Maggie herself. He had never physically assaulted or threatened her, and she didn't know he had a gun.

Although I had worked as an attorney and advocate for women for many years, I too had missed the warning signs in the relationship. My long-standing work to end violence against women became more personal and immediate. I was determined to turn Maggie's tragic death into an opportunity to help other women move on with their lives after abuse as Maggie could not.

In the two decades since Maggie's death, I have worked with hundreds of women who have experienced domestic violence, sexual assault and child abuse and helped them take the journey from victim to survivor to thriver. These women long to move beyond the abuse, violence and trauma in their lives, but they don't know how to make that happen. This is the work I was born to do, and now I do it in Maggie's memory.

The women I have worked with over the years have done remarkable things! They have gone back to school, gotten new, better jobs, started singing again, bought their first homes and most of all, many have found new healthy, loving relationships. They have entered the Thriver Zone and learned how to stay there so they can regain their power and find purpose in living the fabulous life ahead of them in the Thriver Zone. I am so proud of them! But having a positive outlook on life is hard for survivors of abuse and loss. It really gets to us sometimes that everyone else seems to have an easier life, a more comfortable journey or a less challenging existence.

But now I know that the truest measure of our lives is not what we have experienced, but what we have made of our experiences. We don't really know how good it can get once we get positive and focus our energies on our future, not the past. Whatever we might have imagined for ourselves is only a fraction of what we can have when we free ourselves to live well, be happy and create the life we want. Then living well is not only the best revenge; it is, in fact, the song of our soul and the fulfillment of all our dreams.

I hope that this book, the third in *The Thriver Zone Series*™ following *Entering the Thriver Zone: A Seven-Step Guide to Thriving After Abuse* and *Staying in the Thriver Zone: A Road Map to Manifest a Life of Power and Purpose,* will provide you with all you need to find the life of peace, joy and freedom you have always dreamed of as a thriver!

—Susan M. Omilian JD

HOW TO USE THIS BOOK

YES, YOU ARE A WRITER!

You can do the writing exercises in this book that will take you through ***Living in the Thriver Zone: A Celebration of Living Well as the Best Revenge.*** If you are afraid someone might see what you have written, write on a piece of paper and then destroy it. You don't have to keep what you write. Just get it out there for a while and let it shine!

WORKING FROM WRITING PROMPTS IS EASY!

When you see ✒ throughout this book, it means it's time to write from a "writing prompt!" A writing prompt is simply a way into your writing. Let it take you where it will, even if what you write has nothing to do with the prompt. Keep writing. Don't stop! Don't worry about spelling, grammar, or if what you wrote makes any sense! If you like printable copies of the worksheets in this book, go to *www.ThriverZone.com* and click on RESOURCES.

DECORATE YOUR OWN JOURNAL.

Before you start writing, buy yourself a journal or notebook and decorate the cover! Use pictures from magazines or photos from your own life as well as stickers or glitter glue to bling it up! You deserve it! It's your Thriver Zone Journal to write in and keep.

INVITE A FRIEND TO JOIN YOU! FORM A THRIVER GROUP!

Get together with a group of your friends and THRIVE! Visit *ThriverZone.com* to learn how. Find more writing prompts and exercises there. You can work through this book by yourself or invite a friend or group of friends to do it with you. Writing, reading, and sharing the experience with other women is a fabulous thing to do.

THERE ARE NO RULES!

You can't do this wrong! Don't worry—you can do it! Visit *ThriverZone.com* to learn how. You will also find more writing prompts and exercises there. ENJOY!

Getting Started

LIVING YOUR BEST LIFE AS A THRIVER

Thriving. That's fighting.
Surviving is barely getting by.

— Jillian Michaels

Twenty years ago when my nineteen-year-old niece Maggie was killed by her ex-boyfriend, I vowed to work with women to help them take the journey from victim to survivor to thriver as Maggie could not. For twenty years prior to Maggie's senseless death, I was involved in advocating for women's rights and ending violence against women. I represented abused women in divorce cases, founded a sexual assault crisis center and worked on defining sexual harassment in the workplace as a legal cause of action.

So in the last forty years, I have heard a lot of stories from women who have been victims of violence. They have experienced domestic violence, sexual assault and child abuse as well as other horrific acts of abuse and trauma. I have learned how these experiences have impacted their lives and that the impact has been compounded over the years. They have told me how these experiences have derailed them financially, socially and emotionally so that, in many cases, they struggle daily to make a living, feed their children or even dream of having an easier, happier life. Some have told me that they have hardly lived without violence and trauma at any time in their lives, so these impacts have been life-long and overwhelming.

You, too, may be one of these women who has been victimized, traumatized and suffered horribly. But if you are reading this book, you may have at some point courageously taken the first step on the journey beyond abuse. You have broken the silence and spoken up about what happened to you so you could get help.

WARNING SIGNS OF AN UNHEALTHY, ABUSIVE RELATIONSHIP

He is controlling, possessive and overly demanding of her time and attention. He appears at times to be two different people: one, charming, loving and kind; the other, abusive, vicious and mean—like "Dr. Jekyll and Mr. Hyde." He keeps her on edge, not knowing who he'll be. He makes her feel bad about herself and will, at times, be sorry for his behavior, promising not to do it again. But he will do it again and then deny, minimize or blame others for his behavior. She will feel it is all her fault. If only she could please him more or be more compliant, he wouldn't treat her this way.

EMOTIONAL
- He insults her, calls her names and belittles her in private and in public with her family and friends.
- He isolates her from family and friends, forbidding her to see them or limiting her access to them.
- He is jealous of her contact with others, particularly with other men. He exaggerates her relationships with other men, accusing her unfairly of having affairs outside of their relationship.
- He wants to know where she is at all times, calling or texting her to find out who she is with. He invades her privacy by checking her cell phone, viewing her email or monitoring her web pages.
- He refuses to accept when she ends the relationship and may stalk her long afterwards.

PHYSICAL
- He yells, screams and loses his temper easily, sometimes disproportionately over unimportant things.
- He destroys her things, kicks or breaks other property, making her fear that he could hurt her, too.
- He intimidates her, making her afraid of him by his looks, actions and gestures.
- He grabs her, kicks her, slaps her, punches her, strangles her or draws a gun or weapon and threatens to kill her. He harms her pets or threatens to hurt or harm her family or friends.
- He stalks her with unwanted phone calls, visits to her house or job and secretly monitors her actions.

ECONOMIC
- He controls her access to money, even her own money or money she has earned herself.
- He refuses to pay bills or let her know about family income, investments or property.
- He keeps her from getting or keeping a job, refuses to support their family or children.
- He makes all the big decisions, using male privilege to get his way and insisting on rigid gender roles.

PSYCHOLOGICAL
- She feels like she is going crazy, that his view of the world is not reasonable, but she will have little chance of convincing him otherwise and he demands her absolute loyalty to his way of thinking.
- He says he can't live without her or will kill himself if she leaves, so she fears ending the relationship.
- He pushes the relationship too far, too fast and is obsessed with her and wants her for himself.
- He has unrealistic expectations and demands, and she feels it is her fault he's not happy.

SEXUAL
- He demands to have sex forcibly without her consent with him or with others.
- He withdraws sex from her or makes it conditional on her compliance to his demands.
- He calls her crude names, implying she is promiscuous and unfaithful sexually to him.

For more information on the Duluth Power and Control Wheel, see *theduluthmodel.org*.

However, if you are still in crisis or have safety concerns, for immediate crisis intervention services in your local community, call the **National Domestic Violence Hotline 800-799-SAFE (7233)** or **800-787-3224 (TTY for the deaf)** and visit *www.ndvh.org* or the **National Sexual Assault Hotline 800-656-HOPE (4673)**, operated by the **Rape, Abuse & Incest National Network (RAINN)**, and visit *www.rainn.org*.

If you are not sure if you are in an abuse relationship, take a look at the Warning Signs of an Unhealthy Relationship on the previous page.

FROM VICTIM TO SURVIVOR

Even after you have reported the incidents to law enforcement or told your therapist, counselor, advocate or someone you trust so you could get help, you may still be dealing with fear for your own personal safety or that of your children. Most of all, you may just want the abuse to stop and maybe prosecute the offender or file for divorce. But you may also have some of these goals or needs as a survivor of abuse to:

- address impacts of abuse on you or your children
- stabilize your life and that of your children financially, emotionally and socially
- break the cycle of violence in your lives
- have peace, freedom and joy in your life every day

Your desire to address these impacts and stabilize your life may be strong as you move from victim to survivor, but one question I have found often remains. Yes, you may feel safer and more able to cope with daily life despite the immediate concerns above. Yet a part of you – maybe something deep inside – wonders, "Will I be okay? Will I ever feel normal again?" and, most pertinent for our work together here, "I have survived so far, but what's next?"

These questions are frequently asked of me by women who come into the two-day *My Avenging Angel Workshops*™ that I have conducted since 2001 in memory of my niece Maggie. (For more about the workshop program, see *Resources*.) In fact, Jenny, one of the *Thriver Success Stories* in Part Four of this book, asked me that exact question – would she ever be okay again?

Here's how Lora, one of the women from my workshop, described her state of mind when she attended the first workshop session.

I had done a lot work before I met Susan, attempting to make the best of a bad situation, dressing up my existence and trying to make life choices that wouldn't victimize me. I knew I was no longer a victim. I had learned how to manage not to be that, but I was always wearing my "survivor" armor. The armor was heavy, and it defined who I was and my limiting circumstances.

What a wonderful description of the "armor" or shell that you as a survivor may wear as result of what you have endured. As a survivor, you may be heavily burdened with low self-esteem, emotional fear, shame, guilt and hopelessness – the inevitable impacts of being abused and violated in our society today. Those impacts may also include being depressed, appearing lost or suffering from health problems as a result of the assault. But most of you, like Jenny, will probably be deeply worried that your lives will never get any better. In this state of mind, you might believe, like Lora, that the impacts of abuse and violence will forever define your life as limited and permanently damaged.

Sometimes this damage is evident by the looks of pain on our faces or in the way we carry our bodies or talk about the future. We live with the hope that someone, somewhere, can make it all better. We'll even accept a "band-aid" approach, just so the pain, fear and disappointment will stop for some period of time.

VICTIM ⇨ SURVIVOR ⇨ THRIVER

Lora describes how her work with me changed her perception of this part of her journey.

When I went to the first session of Susan's workshop, I didn't know what to expect. My expectations were of an open forum where each of us would tell our stories and grieve our sorry existences together with Susan's support. Luckily, that was not Susan's intention. Susan was simply asking me to remove my armor and consider a part of me untouched by the abuse.

Could this part of me put the abuse aside and motivate me to search for my true passion? I knew this part of myself, not well, but I believed there was a center core that no one had disturbed. Susan encouraged me to invite that part out and talk awhile, dream awhile and grieve our years of separation. Listening to the experiences of others as well was key to opening this part of me.

Getting Started

I call opening up to the part of us that is untouched by the abuse as "finding or making contact with the Happy Person Inside You." We'll explore that part of us later in Part Three of this book as one of the *Seven Steps to Thriving After Abuse* that I have developed as part of my motivational model. We'll focus specifically on *Step Three: Connect with the Happy Person Inside You*, which many women who come to this work find particularly helpful on their journey.

SEVEN STEPS ON THE JOURNEY TO THRIVING AFTER ABUSE

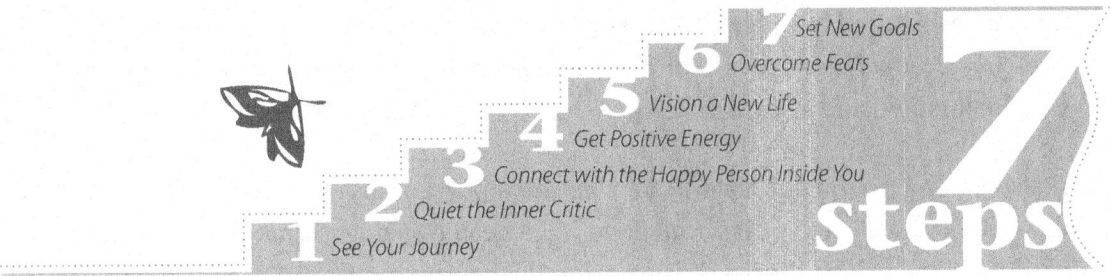

(See my book *Entering the Thriver Zone: A Seven Step Guide to Thriving After Abuse* for more on the Seven Steps with the exercises and work sheets to go with them.)

For now, let me say that in working with hundreds of women since 2001 who have come to my workshops, attended a training or read my books, I have helped them see that they may have lost contact with their Happy Person Inside. They feel lost and alone, overwhelmed and paralyzed by the negativity of the wickedly mean voice of their Inner Critic that is running their lives. They usually express this loss in their lives with the question "Why can't I feel normal again?" but I give them another way to describe what they are really seeking. They want to know if they can reclaim their lives after abuse and achieve some kind of a "new normal" or anything close to it. When I agreed that might be possible, but also suggest that they could even be happy again and feel joy, they look at me incredulously and ask, "Is that really possible?"

But their eyes really shine when I tell them that the *My Avenging Angel Workshops*™ I conduct for women like them are based on the idea that "living well is the best revenge." They like that idea – they like it a lot! "Living well is the best revenge" is a quote attributed to George Herbert that becomes a mantra for the journey beyond abuse. To me, living well means freeing ourselves to live in the present, not the past, by taking the journey beyond surviving to thriving!

FROM SURVIVOR TO THRIVER

What is a "thriver?" It's a new word for most of us, so here's my working definition:

A **"thriver"** is a happy, self-confident and productive individual who believes she has a prosperous life ahead of her. She is primed to follow her dreams, go back to school, find a new job, start her own business or write her story. She believes in herself and in her future so much that she will not return to an abusive relationship. She speaks knowledgeably and confidently about her experiences and is not stuck in her anger or need for revenge. Living well is her best revenge! She has found a network of women who understand and share her desire to move forward after abuse.

I suspect that you might have picked up this book because you were intrigued by the words "Thriver Zone" in the title. You might have been thinking, "What does it mean to be a thriver?" or "I'd like to be a thriver." Most of all, "I'd love to live in the Thriver Zone!"

How to live in the Thriver Zone is what we'll be exploring in this book. I believe it is the end result of a journey beyond abuse and beyond our limited beliefs about ourselves. That includes our narrow expectations of how our future life will turn out given the abuse, violence and trauma we have experienced in our past. We have only thought of ourselves as survivors of abuse at best and have no idea that we could live well or even find our happy ending! That is a pretty dire forecast!

But not to worry! I have imagined this book as presenting some real possibilities for all of us to see for how we can live as thrivers. We have some great role models to celebrate in this book for whom living well has been their best revenge. The stories of the seven women I interviewed for the Thriver Success Stories – I call them Super Hero Thrivers – will tell us about this journey beyond abuse, beyond even surviving, to find a thriving happily-ever-after!

All seven have attended one or more of my workshops over the years, been part of my follow-up group, attended retreats with me and have set and actually accomplished new, exciting goals in their life after abuse. (For more information about the *My Avenging Angel Workshops,*™ the follow-up groups and retreat weekends that I conduct, go to *Resources* in the back of this book.) In Part Four of this book, these amazing women will tell you what being a thriver means to them, what they have they accomplished as a thriver and their goals going forward. You'll learn how they found new vigor, focus and purpose to their lives in being thrivers, not just survivors of abuse. Inspired by their stories, you'll have a chance to write about your own journey beyond abuse in a new and different way.

Watch for this ✎**PROMPT** for the writing exercises in this book!

For now, I'll include a summary here of what being a thriver means to each of the seven women – Adrienne, Cathryn, Jenny, Pamela, Sophia, Tawanda and Tennille – and how they have aspired to become a thriver in their lives.

(See the full story of each women, including their interviews in Part Four of this book.)

Enjoy the positive energy and clear focus reflected in the response of each of these women to the question: "What is a thriver?"

Surviving is essential. Thriving is elegant.
— MAYA ANGELOU

SUMMARY FROM THE THRIVER SUCCESS STORIES

What Being a Thriver Means to Me!

ADRIENNE

I know I am a thriver because I can look at myself the mirror and see a happy face! My eyes are blue again, and there is happiness there now where before there was only gray and sadness. Yes, that's right! My eyes have changed back to their God-given color – blue.

I know I am a thriver because I now feel joy when I wake up in the morning! Joy! Joy! Joy! Joy to be alive, joy to work, joy to see my children grow to be adults.

I know I am a thriver because I see color in the world again! The world is a rainbow!

CATHRYN

Thriving is living within my own personal power while still respecting others. Even if I am angry at those who hurt me, I still choose to treat them with respect and compassion. That is a very important value to me. Thriving means taking care of myself so well that I have energy to take care of others, even those who have hurt me. Feeling compassion for those who hurt me is the ultimate level of thriving to me. It is a level of integrity that comes from being whole.

JENNY

At first, being a thriver was about living in the moment, letting go of what had happened to me in my past and living without fear. Now I feel that thriving is really about living authentically and letting go of the feeling that you have to please people or be worried about how other people feel about you.

PAMELA

Before I came to Susan's workshop, I thought a thriver was someone who had it all together. She was rich, really warm, taking good care of her kids and had every quality you would ever want. Now I think of a thriver as somebody who takes whatever their life gives them – a lot of people have bad things going on – and they just walk through it. They are able to be kind to people along the way, pursue their goals and keep going and trying. Today I can see that I'm getting there as a thriver. I have grown a lot, and I've been trying different things.

SOPHIA

To me, being a thriver is about movement. It is about processing our experiences in life, the good ones as well as the difficult ones, and doing self-reflection so that we can move on to that next level of self-improvement. Just as I have been inspired by those like Susan who have been empowered by the tragedy they have faced, I know that I, too, can be a role model for others by moving beyond the circumstances of my life. I have something I can give back to people who are hurting. We all have something that has caused us pain and trauma and giving back once we move beyond that pain and trauma is our legacy of hope to others.

TAWANDA

Thriving to me is about living beyond the abuse, beyond the pain. Where I am today, compared to three years ago, is like I'm walking on water. Now I believe that there is nothing that can stop me except for me. I still struggle with my Inner Critic and how to keep it quiet, but that battle is nowhere near what it was before. Today I tell myself "I want to do this" and "I can do it." There is no more "Oh, I can't" or "What's someone going to think of me?" if I do this or that. Nope! I'm going for it! I'm doing it! I shortcut all that negative chatter. I have NO time for that anymore! In my journey from survivor to thriver, I have set my goals, kept my energy focused, quieted my Inner Critic and remembered my vision for the future. It feels like I'm living my fantasy in real life! It is so cool! No one else has ever done something like that before!

TENNILLE

Thriving has allowed me to be more forgiving of myself and more compassionate even for people who have abused me. I don't have to hug them or be their friends, but I can and do forgive them with all of my heart. Would saying that make a difference to them? I don't know but saying it for myself makes me feel better when I'm not holding on to all that emotional baggage. Also, letting go of negative thoughts and energy keeps me more in positive energy, something that is very important to me on my journey from survivor to thriver. I need people around me who are positive and supportive.

Here are other comments about thriving from women who have worked with me:

"I am a thriver, a person who can DREAM and take action to be productive. I feel I am becoming myself again. I am overcoming my fears and regaining my voice. Now I know I am not alone. I am allowing myself to love me!" — ***PAM***

"Susan's workshops and materials helped me to come alive and know that I am somebody. I am a thriver!" — ***VONDA***

"Because of Susan, I believe I have a chance to live and thrive after abuse. She has helped me get out of a dark room and see the light." — ***GORDANA***

"Susan is such an inspiration! Her work continues to help women to find their true selves. I will be forever grateful for her being in my life and showing me that I could do this – live the life of a thriver after abuse!" — ***DONNA***

"Susan has been there for me, connected me with other women and encouraged me to seize opportunities to move forward with my life. Her work has helped me focus on my passions without fear and grounded me in a community of strong women who are my role models as I move forward as a thriver." — ***FAYE***

"Susan's work introduced me to a space untouched by the abuse I have experienced. There my Happy Person Inside and I walk hand-in-hand as I rise from survivor to thriver! With all growth, there are many challenges along the way. For me the thought-provoking, soul-searching work and encouragement that Susan has provided made those challenges easier to move through."

— *TERI*

THE JOURNEY OF THIS BOOK

My idea for this third book in *The Thriver Zone Series*™ is to show you how the tools and techniques of the motivational model that I have developed have helped women take the journey beyond abuse so that today they are living in the Thriver Zone. I chose seven women to interview as our Thriver Success Stories so I could find out for you how they did it! (See the interviews with those women in full in Part Four of this book.)

I asked them how "living well is the best revenge" inspired them and how the tools and techniques in my motivational model have helped them to move on from experiencing the most horrific kinds of abuse, degradation and violence to surviving and even thriving! Strong, resilient and determined, they wanted their lives back, and by focusing on the positive and finding power, passion and purpose in their lives, they are getting them back!

Like these women and many others who have attended my workshops or read one or more of my books, you, too, can use the motivational guidance I have developed and included in *The Thriver Zone Series.*™ You can live in the Thriver Zone and celebrate living well as *your* best revenge!

Each part of this book will give you tools and techniques so that you can:

- See yourself as the hero of your own story and answer the Call to Adventure in Part One and become a Super Hero Thriver in Part Two. You can overcome the challenges of your life and reap the reward of finding your true, authentic self – THE REAL YOU!

- Connect with the Happy Person Inside, a part of you untouched by all that has happened to you. Vanquish your Inner Critic's power to sabotage your path forward. We'll review these tools in the *Seven Steps to Thriving After Abuse* and *A Road Map to Manifest a Life of Power and Purpose* in Part Three.

Getting Started

- Learn from the women who share their Thriver Success Stories and serve as Super Hero Thriver role models now living well in the Thriver Zone in Part Four.
- Assemble your *Living in the Thriver Zone* toolbox and have an opportunity to test how well you are living in the Thriver Zone today in Part Five.

Remember: Living well is not only the best revenge, but the song of your soul and the fulfillment of all your dreams. Enjoy the journey!

~ ~ ~ ~ ~ ~ ~ ~ ~ ~ ~ ~ ~ ~ ~ ~ ~

You basically have two choices about how to live your life.
One is to be a survivor and the other is to be a thriver. Be a thriver.

— Thomas Friedman

The only journey is

the one within.

– Rainer Maria Rilke

Part One
TAKE THE JOURNEY

*The only impossible journey
is the one you never began.*

—Tony Robbins

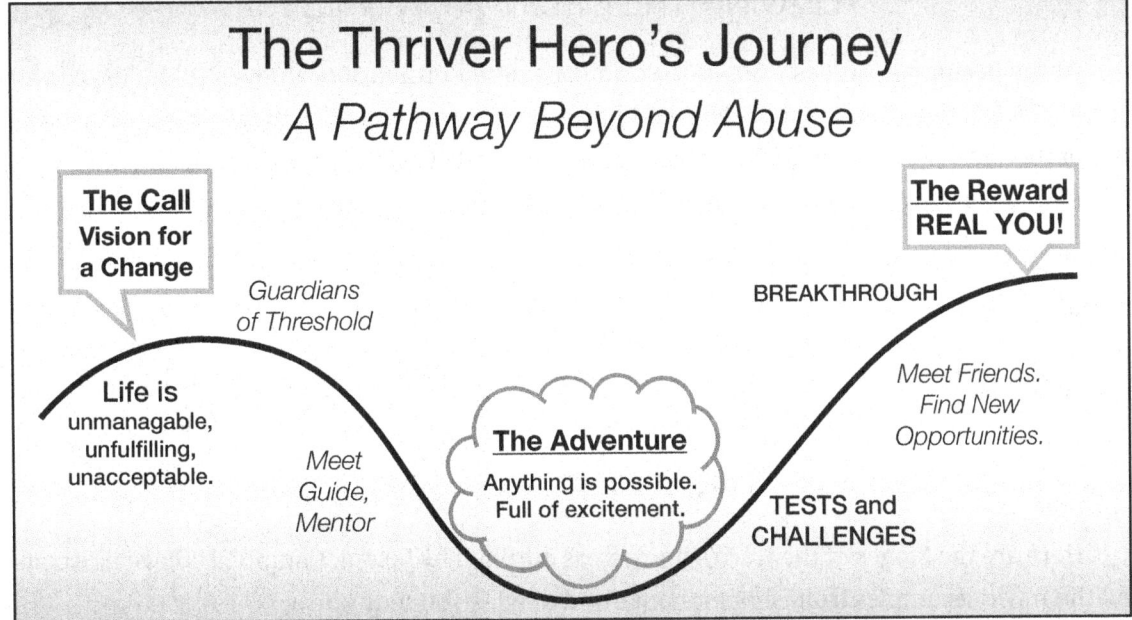

Did you ever think of your life as a journey with you as the hero of it?

You might ask yourself, "Me, a hero? How is that possible?"

What is a hero? I believe a hero is a person who combats adversity through feats of ingenuity, courage or strength. A hero is also resilient and strong, determined and focused. A hero is called to adventure and seeks a reward at the end of that journey.

The journey of the hero, as Joseph Campbell, an American professor who studied stories and myths throughout the world discovered, is a common pattern beneath the narrative elements of all the great myths in our culture, regardless of their country of origin or time of creation. From his studies, Campbell set forth several basic stages of what he saw as the hero's journey and quest.

Popularized in Campbell's book *The Hero with a Thousand Faces,* I believe that this Hero's Journey is adaptable to the quest that women take after they have experienced domestic violence, sexual assault and other abuse in order to reclaim their lives and find their authentic selves.

Intrigued? Let's explore the hero's journey and see how it might apply to our lives.

LEAVING THE ORDINARY WORLD

In the beginning, heroes exist in a world considered ordinary or uneventful by most who live there. Often heroes are considered odd by others in that world or they possess some idea about themselves and their abilities that makes them feel out-of-place. At some point, they may see their ordinary world as unmanageable, dangerous or a place lacking fulfillment for them.

They have a longing for something else to happen, and they don't know how to make it happen.

Example: The Wizard of Oz: Dorothy imagines a world somewhere over the rainbow.
The Greatest Showman (movie): P.T. Barnum rejects his life of poverty.

TAKING THE JOURNEY

Here are the Stages of the Hero's Journey as outlined by Joseph Campbell. I have illustrated them with examples from stories, books and movies you may know.

1) THE CALL TO ADVENTURE

To begin the journey, heroes are called away from ordinary world by a discovery, an event, or some danger. Most don't want to leave ordinary world – home, friends, their lives – to pursue a quest. In the end, they accept their destiny in a moment of choice.

Example: *Wizard of Oz:* a tornado in Kansas sweeps Dorothy away to land of Oz
In *The Greatest Showman* SONG: "This is the Greatest Show"

Heroes can refuse the call to adventure – they are too busy, afraid, overwhelmed.
Example: *Star Wars:* Luke Skywalker refuses the call from Princess Leia, stays on farm to help his aunt and uncle with the harvest until they are killed.

CONFRONTING THE GUARDIAN OF THE THRESHOLD

Forces that stand in your way as you start the journey or occur throughout it can be the gatekeepers, jealous enemies or the hero's own fears and doubts.
INNER CRITIC: I can't have it. I don't deserve it. It's not real.

MEETING GUIDES, MENTORS

This could be a person, an event or the reminder of a set of guiding principles that motivates and encourages hero to go forward and sets a vision for hero to follow. Mentors may guide and help the hero on the journey.
Example: *Cinderella:* fairy godmother
Wizard of Oz: Glinda the Good Witch
The Greatest Showman SONG: "A Million Dreams"

2) THE ADVENTURE

The hero enters a world he or she has never experienced before. There are new rules to learn, new dangers, tests and challenges as well as obstacles and barriers to overcome. The hero must find strength, endurance and mettle to overcome all.

FACING TEST AND CHALLENGES

These tests make the hero stronger and prepare the hero for the breakthrough. When the worst is over, the quest will succeed.
Example: *The Wizard of Oz:* Dorothy defeats the Wicked Witch of the West
The Greatest Showman: Fire destroys circus building; bad publicity

FINDING ALLIES, HELPERS, FRIENDS

The hero needs a sidekick, a fellow traveler or supporters who understand and can help on the journey.

> Example: *Wizard of Oz:* Tinman, Scarecrow and Lion
>> *The Greatest Showman:* The "freaks," "oddities" and circus performers

BREAKTHROUGH OR SUPREME ORDEAL

This is the one thing the hero has journeyed so far to overcome. When the worst has passed, the hero now looks to future.

> Example: *Wizard of Oz:* Dorothy finds the Wizard, but he's a fraud. She learns that she already had everything inside her to get back home to Kansas and the people she loves.
>> *The Greatest Showman:* He learns that family, not money, is most important.

3) THE REWARD – THE REAL YOU! LIVING WELL

The hero is rewarded for her endurance and strength, and she can return "home" with reward in hand. This has been a life-changing journey. She has grown in spirit and has more knowledge about who she is, what her ability and talents are, where she is going with the rest of her life and what she wants to accomplish. Every woman is the hero of her own story!

> Example: *The Greatest Showman* SONG: "From Now On"
>> *Wizard of Oz:* Dorothy wakes from her dream and realizes importance of "home." Learns she must believe in herself and express her inner strength.

YOUR HERO'S JOURNEY TO THRIVING!

You are the hero of your own story from victim to survivor to thriver! Can you see how it unfolds in the stages of the Hero's Journey described above? You have answered (or will answer) the Call to Adventure and leave the Ordinary World to begin your Adventure. Some women I have worked with have written about how they see their journey in heroic terms.

Part One

First, here's Pamela's wonderful and poetic description of her Call to Adventure to come to one of the *My Avenging Angel Workshops*™ that I conduct for women who have experienced abuse. (These are the "angels" she refers to at the end of the piece.)

The Call
by Pamela

She was in shock. She stopped talking, going anywhere. Just sat around partially comatose most of the time. Walked around as if in another world. Shut off her feelings. Kept numb. It didn't happen. She found herself in the hospital. They removed what was detached. It didn't happen. It's Christmas, be happy, go on, forget about it. She pretended a lot. No one knew. Reality was, everyone knew. Most turned their heads, didn't want to get involved; things like that don't happen.

She was aware of every sound. She made sure of her escape route in every room. Protected kids from reality, from force. She prayed, "Let me see what's wrong with me, then I can fix it." One day a note was given to her. On the note was a phone number. A place to call. She thought about it for weeks. She would call today. No, couldn't. She kept the note hidden in her pocket. "Call today!" she would tell herself. "You need to call!" Then things would subside for a while. Garage door opening, everyone scurrying to fix things. Nothing wrong.

"I deserve it," she'd tell herself. She made herself become what he told her she was. That justified it. The unjustifiable, the unexplained. She tried to make sense of it. "I'm sure it happened this way. Well, maybe I'm wrong or I forgot it wasn't that way."

One day she watched her child go through the same scenario. She called. She thought she would get caught. She lied about where she was going. Finally she spoke. She was listened to. It was understood. A glimmer of hope began to get stronger. There were others. They understood. She had help making plans. She met many in secret. Wrote a lot, listened, even talked. As one helper left, she handed her a flyer, saying, "You're ready for this, I think." She called and found herself in a room full of angels. Her journey had just begun.

Here's a piece that another Pam wrote about coming to my workshops, including her Call to Adventure and how she has moved through the other stages of the Hero's Journey.

A Hero's Journey Beyond Abuse
by Pam

I believe my Call to Adventure began when I met Susan. I attended one of her workshops, not knowing what to expect, and I wasn't quite sure where it would lead. At the time, I felt very alone and believed that only the women at the Safe Place understood. But thankfully I had a job, and my son had activities such as Boy Scouts and I had church, so I had to get empowered quickly and get back to life.

I would say that Susan was sorting through how she was might address the murder of her niece Maggie by her ex-boyfriend and I was trying to keep some sanity. But the theme of Susan's workshop, "Living Well Is the Best Revenge," stayed with me. The writing exercises she introduced to us also gave me something that truly helped me calm down my Inner Critic.

On this adventure, I've had "ups" and I've had "downs," and I've met some great friends. I do not have all that I want and need right now, but for all intents and purposes, my children are grown. My weekends at the retreat center with Susan's group have brought me joy, peace, fun, relaxation, and a humbleness. Dreams have been reborn there!

Thank you, Susan and the My Avenging Angel Workshops™, *for saving my life. My children were the reason I left the abuse, but I stand here as a HERO because Susan saw my potential. I am learning day by day – slowly – how to love me.*

I am a thriver, a person who can DREAM and take action to be productive. I feel I am becoming myself again. I am overcoming my fears and regaining my voice. Now I know that domestic violence is not new, and I am not alone. I am allowing myself to love me!

Part One

Here's a piece written by Christine at the annual retreat weekend that I conduct for the women in my follow-up group who have completed both sessions of the *My Avenging Angel Workshops*™ At this retreat, I introduced Joseph Campbell's Stages of the Hero's Journey.

I am the Hero of My Story
by Christine

I met Susan Omilian in 2005 when I attended one of her My Avenging Angel Workshops™ *based on the idea that living well is the best revenge. I hoped that Susan and her workshops could help me find a way beyond the abuse in my life. After attending both sessions of the workshop, I was invited to Susan's follow-up Archangel group along with the other women who had gone through the same or similar types of abuse that I had.*

At one of our weekend retreats Susan conducts annually for her Archangel group, Susan told us about the Hero's Journey and how it starts with the "Call to Adventure." Then she told us we were the heroes of our own stories and that we were to write about being the hero of our lives. I was surprised by the thought that I could be my own hero. I didn't feel like I had done anything in my life to justify being a hero, but then I got to thinking about that Call to Adventure. When did I first answer the Call – or did the Call find me?

You see, for many years I had weathered every storm. I had two abusive husbands and a mother whose treatment of me was abusive. With all those experiences, I learned how to stay strong, not to let them see my tears and don't show them they hurt me with their negative and discouraging words. I had endured abuse in all its forms – verbal, mental and physical – along with isolation and abandonment. It was all done in secret, with no one stepping in to help me. Yet I was the one who felt it was my fault and if I would just try harder, I would be less inadequate. My body, soul and mind were devastated by every word said to me, while the physical and sexual abuse drained my energy. I lost my soul. My mind was confused, and I had no sense of myself.

What I had been battling for many years was hard, but I believed that it was going to get better. But how and when? I didn't know the answer to that until Susan helped me see that I was on a hero's journey from victim to survivor to thriver. My Call to Adventure was to take that journey, walk on my own two feet down the path beyond violence and face the challenges of my life. Susan's group became my friends and allies on this journey who, along with my therapist and support groups, helped me find the strength and courage I needed to move forward in my life with more confidence. The women in Susan's group are upbeat, positive and love to be creative with art, singing and dancing.

One weekend each year, Susan's group spends time at a retreat center on the Connecticut shoreline where we stay in a beautiful house right on the beach. There I feel what it is like to be rich, if only for the weekend! I love sitting out on the beach, listening to the ocean waves, watching the seagulls flying over the waters and feeling the warmth of the sun shining down on me. Then I walk the beach, looking for sea glass and seashells while the ocean water cleanses my soul and takes away the black clouds that at times have followed me everywhere. That place always puts a smile on my face and a quicker stride to my walk that wasn't been there for many years. You could say, like the series on TV, I was Touched by an Angel. Or was it the Archangels of Susan's group?

With the Archangels, we share the positive things in our life, play with each other like children do. We like blowing bubbles, lighting sparklers, wading in the ocean with our clothes on or going to a movie in town with our PJs on and no underwear. We help an angel learn to swim, and we are happy and cry with her when she succeeds. We make ice-cream sundaes at night and watch movies with our PJs on while eating popcorn and breaking our diets. We sing and dance, floating around the floor with scarves as our playthings. We giggle and decorate envelopes and fill them with writing about our weekend that Susan will send to us six months later, and we'll be so surprised when we receive them in the mail.

Joy for me is painting the landscape of the water, sand and the trees in front of me on canvas boards and taking the pictures home to frame, hoping they will allow me to remember even a little bit of how wonderful my time there on the beach is. There we have fun, relax together and forget our financial troubles, our children and what we endured in the past from our abusive ex-husbands.

Today, I help others through my cable television show Beyond Violence and the documentaries I've filmed, including Breaking These Chains of Silence, about the women – the thrivers – who inspire others to take the journey and get to a different place in their life.

Living well is our best revenge! Now I am that strong, independent, and empowered woman who has found her voice with a paintbrush in her hand.

For the Angels
by Christine

Roaring and riding on a storm
Blinded by the wind, rain and darkness
Trembling from the coldness of night,
Night Rider, are you going forward into the Light
Toward your friends, or are you going to return back
Into your Dark, Cold, Comfort Zone you know so well?
The next day would greet me
With a Rainbow of Colors in the Morning Rise
The Clouds show the Pathway to the future.
I'm ready to welcome the unknown onward future
In the warmth of the Angels
In the Songs of the Ocean Waves and Wind.
God always draws us closer to Him.

CALL TO ADVENTURE

A Thriver Hero's Journey

Are you ready to see your story as a hero's journey beyond abuse using Joseph Campbell's stages?

✒ PROMPT: Write about your journey beyond abuse with you as the hero of the story.

You can use the worksheet on the next page with prompts that guide you through each stage of Joseph Campbell's Hero's Journey. Write about how it felt, what held you back from taking the journey and what moved you forward. Maybe it's continuing today; write about that too! Following the worksheet, you'll find a story by Faye, one of the women I have worked with for a number of years who wrote her story using the worksheet prompts.

Make your story big and bold! You are the hero of it

A Call to Adventure: A Thriver Hero's Journey

✒ **PROMPT:** *You are the hero of your journey from VICTIM to SURVIVOR to THRIVER! Complete the sentences below in your journal or notebook.*

LEAVING THE ORDINARY WORLD

It was hard to want to make a change because...

MY CALL TO ADVENTURE (e.g., an event, person or feeling)

I felt something needed to change...

I answered the call when I...

OR I resisted that change, refused the call until I...

Confronting the Guardians of the Threshold

I felt something holding me back from making that change...

There were negative voices in my head telling me...

But I decided not to listen to them by...

MY ADVENTURE

At first, I believed that anything is possible, full of excitement because

I felt that I could...

Then I had these tests and challenges...

I faced these tests and challenges by doing...

MY ALLIES Friends, Helpers showed up! These people helped me to...

The day I broke through and felt it was all worth it because I could feel...

I accomplished so much, including these things I thought I couldn't do...

THE REAL YOU! THE REWARD – CELEBRATION

Because of this journey, I proved to myself and others that I am... My life has changed because of this journey in this way...

TODAY I celebrate my life by living well as my best revenge because now I can...

MY THRIVER HERO'S JOURNEY STORY
by Faye

LEAVING THE ORDINARY WORLD

It was hard to want to make a change and leave my marriage because I had children who depended on me. Also, I am a business owner, and I need to stay focused and alert. My job as a day-care provider requires a lot of emotional and physical exertion. Many people, including a lot of children and their parents, depend on me. To take on another adventure was just too overwhelming.

MY CALL TO ADVENTURE

But I felt that something needed to change. I found myself very unhappy in a bad marriage, and I stopped doing anything for myself. I saw the effect that this kind of negativity was having on me and my children, and I knew I couldn't stay in that situation.

I answered the call to end my marriage when I understood that my life was not anywhere I wanted it to be. Bad feelings were now engulfing me. I knew I wouldn't be any good to or for anyone if this situation continued. A part of me – a major part – was lost and missing. I wasn't a whole person anymore.

I resisted that change, refused the call for a very long time, probably ten to twelve years. When I had my third child, things were so out of control, but still it took me seven years to take the first steps.

Confronting the Guardians of the Threshold

What held me back from making that change were my strong beliefs about family life. I always wanted that happy, healthy family I had dreamed about since I was a child. Who was I to break up this family, even if it wasn't healthy for me to stay there?

There were negative voices in my head telling me I couldn't make it on my own. It wasn't right to separate my family. I didn't deserve to be happy. I even thought that maybe, somehow, I had caused this unhappy life.

But I decided not to listen to those voices, and I looked deep within myself to find what really mattered to me. I reached out to God, to the Universe and, to my surprise, even to friends who I thought were no longer there for me.

MY ADVENTURE

At first, I thought that maybe I could be happy; maybe I wouldn't have to live with the ugly feelings that had encompassed me. Maybe I would be able to be lighthearted again. Maybe I could smile more and even be playful. Maybe I could do the things I had wanted to do for a long time and reach some of my goals.

Then I had these tests and challenges. Money! That's always a hard step to figure out. I had to budget more efficiently and stretch the money I was able to earn myself. But I didn't want to take away from my children or limit their experiences in life. I had to meet their needs and even get some of their wants met. Another challenge was filing for the divorce from my husband, going through the court system, filling out papers, finding a lawyer and raising the money to fund the divorce.

I faced these tests and challenges by joining several support groups and educating myself on budgeting and finances.

MY ALLIES and FRIENDS

Friends, Helpers showed up! They helped me to give value back to myself. They validated my feelings, and even strangers who were positive toward me helped me to be strong. A smile and a kind word can lift you up so much.

What I realize today is that even though I have come so far, I feel that I have only partially broken through. My journey has, at times, been very overwhelming. As I made a choice to follow a certain path, other things were always happening. Life doesn't stand still even as you try to heal. I've had to consistently reassess my plans and choices, re-configure where I was going in my life and what I really wanted. My beliefs of what a family should be about were really not so far off. I am a good mother. I care about and feel so much for all the people in my life – my children, my grandbabies, my day-care kids and families, my relatives and my friends. Every day my tribe grows bigger and bigger. Today, I do have a large, happy family, but I can see that I only started out with the wrong partner. My family grows stronger, healthier and happier every day.

Part One

THIS IS ME! The Reward – Celebration

Because of this journey, I proved to myself and others that I am strong, resourceful, determined, loving and loveable. I am also enough and worth it! I am kind and loyal, and I have met some very amazing people who reflect my beliefs. They only make me feel stronger. Many people have come to me and said very kind and uplifting words to me. This has helped me continue on my journey to become independent.

My life has changed because of this journey, but I see that I still hesitate in making decisions, not because I think I don't deserve goodness and happiness. It is more because so much is flowing within me as to what I want to do and where I want to go. It's still all so fluid, and yet every day the vision for my life gets clearer.

TODAY I celebrate my life by living well as my best revenge because now I can do anything I set my mind to! I can find the resources that I need to move forward. I have learned to speak up and ask for help. If I become sad or any negativity tries to enter into my soul again, I know I can make the choice not to stay there long or not at all. Today, I keep moving, striving and thriving!

— *Faye*

You are the hero of your own story.
The privilege of a lifetime is being who you are.

— JOSEPH CAMPBELL

An interesting journey

never follows a straight path.

– Marjan Van Den Belt

Part Two

BE A SUPER HERO THRIVER!

*A hero is an ordinary individual who finds the strength
to persevere and endure in spite of overwhelming obstacles.*

— CHRISTOPHER REEVE

I am a Super Hero Thriver!

my power

my purpose my passion!

Super Hero Thrivers are everywhere! I have met them, and I am amazed!

Over the last twenty years of conducting *My Avenging Angel Workshops*™ based on the idea that "living well is the best revenge" and developing a motivational model for women who have survived abuse for the books in *The Thriver Zone Series*™, I have worked with hundreds of women who have experienced domestic violence, sexual assault, child abuse and other kinds of violence and trauma. I also have done trainings for survivors and providers of services based on the model in a variety of settings, including domestic violence and sexual assault crisis centers, mental health clinics, victim advocacy organizations, hospitals, prisons (with both male and female inmates) and Indian tribes. (See more about my trainings in *Resources* at back of this book.)

From the stories I have heard from these women, not only of what has happened to them, but also what it took for them to move from survivors to thrivers, they all should, in my estimation, be celebrated as Super Hero Thrivers. But there are not enough pages in this book to do justice to them and their journeys beyond abuse.

For some, it is a story of sheer survival. Just getting out alive was a miracle. My niece Maggie did not. She lost her life to this violence and will never return to my life or our family. I know telling her story wherever I have gone over these last twenty years has inspired women to move beyond abuse as Maggie could not. Then the story becomes not just how you survived, but also how you took the critical "next-step" to thriving and reclaiming your life.

FINDING THE SUPER HERO THRIVER INSIDE YOU

One of the first things I suggest to women who want to tell their stories of the journey beyond abuse is that what most people want to know is not so much about what happened to you on your journey from victim to survivor. They may be sorry that all that happened to you, but what they really want to know is: How did you get from survivor to thriver? That part of the story has the most value to a woman who is on her own journey, and if she is asking you, she's probably at the beginning of it.

She'll want to know: "Will I really be okay after all this?"
She'll want to know: "Will I ever be normal again – however I define that term?"
She'll want to know: "Will I ever be able to let go of my past?"
Most of all, she will want to know if living well really is the best revenge.

My questions to the seven women – the Super Hero Thrivers I interviewed for this book– were definitely along those lines. (See the full list of questions I asked them in Part Four.)

First of all, I wanted to know how they saw themselves when they first came to one of the *My Avenging Angel Workshops*™ and how the motivational model I have developed through conducting the workshops has helped them. This model includes *Seven Steps to Thriving* and *A Road Map to Manifest a Life of Power and Purpose*, which will be reviewed in Part Three.

Second, which exercises in my motivational model helped them the most?

Third, how do they see themselves as thrivers today? How has adding the word thriver to their vocabulary helped them on their journey beyond abuse?

Fourth, has living well been their best revenge? What does living well mean to them? Do they see a life of power and purpose for themselves emerging from their experiences?

In Part Four of this book, you'll be able to read in depth how each of the seven women I interviewed answered these questions and more! For now, let me summarize here their answers to one question: "When you first came into Susan's workshop, how were you feeling about yourself and your future?"

SUMMARY FROM THE THRIVER SUCCESS STORIES

FROM THE BEGINNING

When I first met Susan, I was really very good at surviving, but not much more than that. In fact, I was a "high-functioning" survivor. It might have felt like I was moving forward, but actually I was vacillating between victim and survivor. I didn't even know what "thriving" was. **– Adrienne**

Coming into Susan's workshop for first time, I didn't feel so good about myself. So many people's words had beaten me down for so long. I certainly wasn't thriving – I wasn't full of joy for life. **– Cathryn**

The one thing I remember about coming to Susan's workshop was how I was struggling with the symptoms of Post-Traumatic Stress Disorder (PTSD) at the time. I was functioning though, so every therapist I went to told me, "Oh! You're fine." But I didn't feel fine, and I didn't want to live like this anymore. It was one of the darkest times I ever remember living through. **– Jenny**

When first met Susan, I didn't see any future ahead of me. I had no dreams about what I wanted to be in my life. I had a tiny bit of hope, but not a lot. Hope means to me that something good is coming and you can start to see that there are possibilities out there. But I had very little hope. **– Pamela**

When I came into Susan's workshop for the first time, it was a cold winter day in January, and I was broken. It felt like I was coming to a place of refuge, someplace better than where I was, and I needed someone there to tell me that I deserved better. **– Sophia**

When I first met Susan, I wasn't feeling too good about myself. I was in a very toxic, abusive relationship, and I felt trapped there without a real future ahead of me. I guess I was looking for some kind of change in my life, but I wasn't sure I was ready for that. I wasn't sure that I could do it. **– Tawanda**

I was feeling okay about myself when I first came to Susan's workshop. I was feeling okay about myself until Susan wrote "VICTIM to SURVIVOR to THRIVER" on the board and talked about how the journey beyond abuse was from struggle to transformation to happy ending. It was then that I realized I wasn't living in my happy ending but stuck somewhere in between victim and survivor. **– Tennille**

Maybe that's how you felt when you first came across the motivational model I developed from my workshops and have included in the first two books of *The Thriver Zone Series*™. Or maybe that's how you are feeling right now as you are reading this book, realizing that you aren't living your best life ever after abuse. You, like some of the women above have described, may be merely surviving or vacillating between survivor and thriver.

Let's see how we can get you on that journey to thriving as soon as possible!

In Part Three of this book, we'll review some tools for taking the journey beyond abuse that are in my motivational model and laid out in my first two books, *Entering the Thriver Zone* and *Staying in the Thriver Zone*. But before that, let's set a Super Hero Thriver vision that can propel you forward whether you're just starting or continuing on your journey beyond abuse. Didn't you always want to be a Super Hero? With that kind of super energy plus my tools in your hands, you'll be taking your hero's journey from victim to survivor to thriver at super speed!

Part Two

BE A SUPER HERO THRIVER!

As I have described earlier in this book, the women who attend the *My Avenging Angel Workshops*™ have also been invited to attend an annual retreat weekend at a beach house on Connecticut's shoreline. At a recent retreat weekend, our theme was "Superwoman," and we spent the weekend focused on the Super Hero inside us. Our theme song was "Superwoman" by Alicia Keyes. (Check out this song and the official music video for it. It's great!) At the retreat, we made and put on our Superwoman capes, shields and headbands. Then we explored the Superwoman image and what kind of superpowers we'll need on our Hero's Journey to thriving.

On the next page, set your own vision for your Super Hero Power, Passion and Purpose.

Think about Power as – Courage, Strength, Positive Energy, Being Open, Empowered.

Think about Passion as – Readiness, Flow, Rebirth, Hope, Excitement, Potential.

Think about Purpose as – Connection, Cause, Discovery, Motivation, Force for Good.

I've also included sample writings from two of the women in my follow-up group, as well as one that I wrote about being a Superwoman.

Let's see what you can do with this writing exercise! Review and complete the writing prompts in the worksheet and then write a paragraph in your journal or notebook about your vision for your life.

Have fun! You are a Super Hero Thriver!

It's not who I am underneath, but what I do that defines me.
— Batman

You are much stronger than you think you are. Trust me.
—Superman

I accept the fact that tomorrow will come and I'm going to rise to meet it.
—Wonder Girl

Living in the Thriver Zone

I AM A SUPER HERO THRIVER!

I Have a Power – I am in control of my life. I am moving forward.

I Have a Passion – I am dedicated to an issue or an idea.

I Have a Purpose – I have a reason for living. There are people and things I care about.

PROMPT: Write down what a hero is to you. *(See definition below.)*

WHAT IS A HERO? – *"A hero ventures forth from the world of common day into a region of supernatural wonder. Fabulous forces are there encountered and a decisive victory is won. The hero comes back from this mysterious adventure with the power to bestow rewards and benefits of this journey on others and to inspire them."*

– Joseph Campbell in *The Hero with a Thousand Faces*

PROMPT: Who is your favorite Super Hero?

You can pick a fictional super hero like Superwoman or Wonder Woman or someone you know in your family or community.

PROMPT: What powers does a Super Hero have? Could you have that power? Could you use that power to do something you thought you couldn't do?

PROMPT: What interests excite you? What causes have you fought for? What are your passions? Could a passion or cause create a purpose for your life?

PROMPT: Describe the world you would like to live in with your Super Hero's power, passions and purpose. What tools would you need to get there?

PROMPT: How can you keep your Super Hero powers going forward to fulfill your purpose in life?

PROMPT: Now write a paragraph with you as the Super Hero describing your powers, purpose and passion. Make it big and bold! Give yourself a name!

Start with "I am a Super Hero! My name is _____."

Part Two

SAMPLE WRITINGS!

Here's the piece that I wrote using the above Super Hero Thriver prompts. I chose Superwoman as my favorite Super Hero. Next are three pieces from women in my follow-up group. Two also selected Superwoman as their Super Hero; the other took another course.

Enjoy the energy, passion and vision of these pieces in writing your own!

I am Superwoman. My name is Sassy Susan!

I will use my power for good to help women thrive after abuse. There is no choice in the matter. This is the work I am supposed to do. The time is now. I can't go back, and I can't not do this. All is well. I am empowered. Everything is within my grasp. If I lose my power, I feel weak and get depressed. But I can keep myself grounded, positive and happy. I will work at it EVERY DAY! I love being a Super Hero.

I am a Superwoman!

– **Susan**

I am Superwoman, and I am using my power to help other survivors and victims of abuse see that they have the strength and courage to leave and make a better life for themselves and their children. We all have the potential to be thrivers, but we need someone to guide us and to be a role model. Since I have walked in their shoes, I can be an example for women who have experienced domestic violence, showing them that they, too, can move beyond the abuse in their lives, not only surviving but thriving! If I can become a thriver after enduring a very abusive marriage, anyone can!

I intend to help everyone I can to move their life toward healing. I will keep my power by continuing to be part of the change the world needs. I will live my life honestly with respect for all. I will continue to volunteer and reach out to everyone I can to educate them about violence from my experience and education. God kept me alive for a reason, and I believe it was to help others out of abusive relationships and on to the journey beyond abuse.

I am a Superwoman!

– **Gaylene**

I am a Superwoman, and I will use my power to create a more peaceful, loving and accepting world. I will begin by transforming my inner self, then my home, then I will go out to the larger community. I have the strength and courage to dance to the rhythms of my soul. I have learned to harness the energy of the hurt, anger, rage and betrayal into a channel of transformation. I will be true to myself and others.

I will keep my superwoman powers by honoring myself in all ways. I will seek out people, places and things that are healthy and life-giving. I will not engage in shame or blame. I will speak my truth at all times. I am learning from workshops on women's issues and rights and I am following a blended spiritual path. I am willing to stand alone and empty at times but also be embraced by the knowledge that I am in a learning, reflective time of my life. I will emerge with quiet strength and radiant grace.

I am a Superwoman!

– **Karen**

I am a Super Hero. My purpose is to save the animals and the planet.

I spread awareness of the importance of using recyclable products and how this change can help our planet. I will use my superpowers to clean up the garbage in the sea and other places on the planet. I'll make plant-based products – utensils, clothing and cleaning supplies – as well as an oil substitute and gasoline replacement. When we make these changes, we won't have to rely on animals for products, and there will be no need to kill them for fur, for meat or for anything.

I have a passion to save the animals because they don't have a voice and their plight is not being heard. They are being slaughtered for their meat, skin and feathers while their homes are being destroyed for paper, wood and access to land. Animals are more vulnerable without their homes. They need our help!

I am a Super Hero!

– **Mallory**

What's next? You may already be familiar with the *Seven Steps to Thriving After Abuse* and *A Road Map to Manifesting a Life of Power and Purpose* that are included in *The Thriver Zone Series*™ books. If not, we'll review both in the next part of this book. Join us!

These tools along with your Super Hero Power, Passion and Purpose we explored in this Part of the book, will give you the courage, strength and determination to find what being a thriver means to you.

Remember our working definition of a thriver from earlier in this book.

A "**thriver**" is a happy, self-confident and productive individual who believes she has a prosperous life ahead of her. She is primed to follow her dreams, go back to school, find a new job, start her own business or write her story. She believes in herself and in her future so much that she will not return to an abusive relationship. She speaks knowledgeably and confidently about her experiences and is not stuck in her anger or need for revenge. Living well is her best revenge! She has found a network of women who understand and share her desire to move forward after abuse.

I call it a "working" definition because I don't think that we've made our idea of what a thriver is big enough yet. I believe that we really don't know how good it can get once we get positive and focus our energies on the future, not the past. Whatever we might have imagined for ourselves is only a fraction of what we can have when we free ourselves to live well, be happy and create the life we want.

So let's go for it! Take the Super Hero energy from this Part of the book and add it to the Thriver Tools that we'll explore in the next Part. Let's see what kind of life we can create for ourselves and those around us as SUPER HERO THRIVERS reclaiming our lives after abuse!

~ ~ ~ ~ ~ ~ ~ ~ ~ ~ ~ ~ ~ ~ ~ ~ ~

This is your life.
You are meant to be its hero.

— Rachel Hollis

The hero's journey is inside you;

Tear off the veils and

Open the mystery of yourself.

— Joseph Campbell

Part Three

FIND TOOLS FOR YOUR JOURNEY

*Be bold; be brave enough
to be your true self.*

— Queen Latifah

VICTIM ⇨ **SURVIVOR** ⇨ **THRIVER**

Congratulations! You are on a journey from victim to survivor to thriver!

Over the last twenty years, I have worked with hundreds of women like you who describe themselves as survivors of abuse, but like you, many of them are ready to take the journey from survivor to thriver. Welcome to the club!

Each time they are given the choice of reliving the abuse and the pain inflicted on them or reaching deep down inside to uncover their true heart's desires, they choose the latter. They have set goals for themselves that they have not only achieved, but also have spurred them on to bigger and better changes for themselves and their children. They have done, in many cases, what they thought was unimaginable! They have reclaimed their lives after abuse and permanently broken the cycle of violence in their lives.

Many of these women will tell you that I, Susan Omilian, did this for them, but I don't think that is true. What they have accomplished and how they see themselves today as thrivers is all about their own hard work and determination. How I have been able to help them do the impossible (as they may describe it at the start) is that I have developed, with their feedback and assistance over the years, some tools for this journey beyond abuse.

For these tools I will take credit, but what they have done with them is all theirs to claim.

You'll see proof of that in the amazing Thriver Success Stories to come in Part Four of this book. For now, let's review those tools so you can see how our Super Hero Thrivers have made them their own.

EXERCISE: WHERE ARE YOU ON YOUR JOURNEY

The first thing I want to know about the women I work with – and what you'll want to know if you are starting here – is where you are stuck right now that keeps you from taking the journey from survivor to thriver? In my experience, the first place to look to find that answer is whether you have some limiting beliefs about yourself and your ability to leave behind you what has happened in the past.

They could be ideas or beliefs about yourself that you've held ever since childhood or ideas or beliefs might also have been fed to you or reinforced while you were in a verbally or psychologically abusive relationship as an adult. In any case, they may be holding you back.

Whether you have just found this book or you have read the other books I have written in *The Thriver Zone Series*™, you may already be moving from survivor to thriver. But it would be good to find out what may be holding you back from fully being in that Thriver Zone, influencing and coloring your thoughts about your present circumstances or your possibilities for the future. The survey I have developed can help you do that. If you have filled in out in the past, do it again now and it will allow you to see how you have been managing these thoughts and beliefs.

The survey is designed to do all of that and more! Read through it on the next page and choose quickly between ALWAYS, SOMETIMES or NEVER Feel This Way. Don't think about it too much. Let the answer come from your heart, not your head. See what you can learn about yourself today and measure it against what you might have thought in the past. You are making progress, so let's find out how much!

SURVEY FOR JOURNEY TO THRIVING

Always feel this way	Sometimes feel this way	Never feel this way	
			I'm too busy for quiet time to think about where I'm going.
			There is no way I can create the life I want right now.
			There are some voices inside my head that are very critical of me, and I'll never get them to quiet down.
			Sometimes I feel there's a happy person inside of me who wants to get out.
			My biggest fear is that I'll never get my life together.
			Bad things always seem to happen to me.
			I'll never figure out who I am or what I want to be when I grow up.
			I don't take any big risks. Life is too scary.
			Abuse has always been in my life. I can't do much about it.
			It's hard to find other people who have gone through what I have and want to change their lives.
			Taking time for me is a selfish thing to do.

If I could change one thing about my life, I'd …

If I had $10 million and all the time to do whatever I wanted, I'd …

Living in the Thriver Zone | *Survey for the Journey to the Thriving* © 2020 by Susan M. Omilian

47

REVIEW YOUR RESULTS

Let's look at what you came up with on the survey. Was any particular statement difficult for you to answer?

Which statements were easiest for you to answer?

✒ PROMPT: Write about that now in your journal or notebook.

In what areas did you mark that you "ALWAYS feel this way"? Any surprises?

Look at your SOMETIMES responses. Are they in areas that you feel you might be able to move into the ALWAYS category? What would be your barriers to doing so?

✒ PROMPT: Write about that now in your journal or notebook.

Now let's review your answer to the question "If I had 10 million dollars and all the time to do whatever I wanted to do, I'd…"

Did anything surprise you there? How possible is that dream for you? What are the obstacles besides time and money? How would it feel to fulfill these dreams?

✒ PROMPT: Write about that now in your journal or notebook.

LOOK AT YOUR BELIEFS ABOUT YOURSELF

Have you noticed that the statements on this survey are all limiting beliefs about yourself and the impact of abuse on your life? What the survey actually measures is your self-esteem –how you feel about yourself and your future. Our view of ourselves rises and falls with the experiences we face in life. This survey helps identify the areas you might want to work on.

For example:

If you checked any of these in the "ALWAYS" or "SOMETIMES" box:

I'm too busy for quiet time to think about where I'm going.

Taking time for me is a selfish thing to do.

> *It's hard to find other people who've gone through what I have and want to change their lives.*

– you may have some limiting beliefs about taking time for yourself – self-care – and finding others who are also moving from survivor to thriver to support you.

✎ **PROMPT:** Write about what you can do to find that kind of support.

If you marked ALWAYS or SOMETIMES for:

> *There are some voices inside my head that are very critical of me, and I'll never get them to quiet down.*

– check out Step 2: *Quiet the Inner Critic* in my *Seven Steps to Thriving After Abuse.*

You can quiet the chatter and use affirmations to substitute negative self-talk with positive! Of all the steps, the women who I've worked with tell me that this is the one they come back to most.

If you checked off this one as NEVER:

> *Sometimes I feel there's a happy person inside of me who wants to get out.*

– be sure to review Step 4, *Connect with the Happy Person Inside.*

Even if you answered SOMETIMES or ALWAYS to this one, you will be connecting with the Happy Person Inside You later which is a key tool for you for living in the Thriver Zone.

All Seven Steps will be reviewed in Part Four of this book.

TAKE SURVEY REGULARLY – Like Our Super Hero Thrivers!

Think about this survey as a way to assess your progress on your journey to thriving and your ability to live in the Thriver Zone full-time! You'll want to see if there is a shift in your attitudes and perceptions of yourself and your future and a stronger belief that you can move forward after abuse.

As I outlined above, some of that movement forward into the Thriver Zone can be accelerated by using the *Seven Steps to Thriving After Abuse* and *A Road Map to Manifest a Life of Power and Purpose,* both of which are tools I have developed in my motivational model. We'll review those tools next, but before we do, check out the progress made by some of the seven women Thriver Success Stories. (See Part Four for full interviews.)

When I asked these women after I interviewed them to do the survey again, the results were quite astonishing. They had moved away from several of the limiting beliefs about themselves that could hold them back from living more permanently in the Thriver Zone.

- Not surprisingly, none of the women marked "ALWAYS Feel This Way" for any of the statements on the survey – except for one. They ALWAYS feel that there is a Happy Person Inside who wants to get out! Excellent!

- Most marked "NEVER Feel This Way" more times than "SOMETIMES Feel This Way" for all the statements, including that they NEVER feel "My biggest fear is that I'll never get my life together" and "Bad things always seem to happen to me."

- One statement they all agreed that they NEVER feel this way anymore was "It's hard to find other people who've gone through what I have and want to change their lives." That means these women have found a Thriver Community that supports and understands their journey moving beyond abuse.

In my interviews with these women in Part Four of the book, you will see that they all agreed that the tools in *The Thriver Zone Series*™ motivational model I have developed have been very helpful to them on their journey to thriving! Let's review both tool sets along with some new materials and sample writings that have prepared especially for you in this book. Enjoy!

~ ~ ~ ~ ~ ~ ~ ~ ~ ~ ~ ~ ~ ~ ~ ~

Within you is a tool box—a box of possibility and hope.
There you will find principles that will transform your life.
— GREG BARRETTE

Part Three

SEVEN STEPS ON THE JOURNEY TO THRIVING AFTER ABUSE

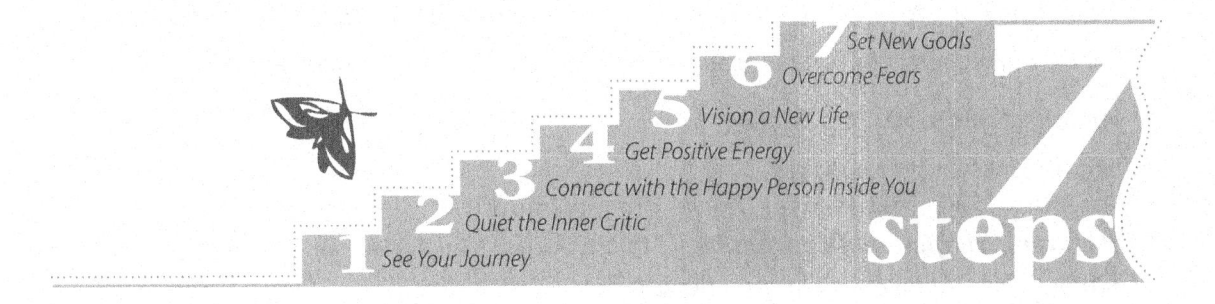

Steps:
1. See Your Journey
2. Quiet the Inner Critic
3. Connect with the Happy Person Inside You
4. Get Positive Energy
5. Vision a New Life
6. Overcome Fears
7. Set New Goals

FIRST TOOL: THE SEVEN STEPS TO THRIVING DO WORK

*Take the first step in faith. You don't have to see
the whole staircase. Just take the first step.*

— MARTIN LUTHER KING JR.

Over the last twenty years, I developed the *Seven Steps to Thriving After Abuse,* and in 2016, I published my first book in *The Thriver Zone Series*™ entitled *Entering the Thriver Zone: A Seven-Step Guide to Thriving After Abuse.* In that book, I laid out the steps one by one with writing exercises, prompts and sample writings. Since then, I have continued to work with women to find different ways to make the steps come alive so they understand them and won't forget to use them. At a recent retreat weekend, I asked the women in my follow-up group to identify what feelings they had before and after using each step and what associations they had with the energy of each step. We also brainstormed stones, stories, songs and images that help us embrace each step in a stronger and more enduring way.

When I asked the women what steps they use most frequently and which help keep them in the Thriver Zone, they told me *Step Two: Quiet the Inner Critic* and *Step Three: Connect with the Happy Person Inside You.* That answer seems to suggest that to live in the Thriver Zone, we most need to keep the negative voices in head quiet and bring up more of the positive. To help with that, I've included some tips from one of the women on how to Quiet the Inner Critic, as well as more sample writings from them on how they have been able to Connect with the Happy Person Inside.

Let's review the Seven Steps here with these new insights and suggestions for you.

STEP 1: SEE YOUR JOURNEY

Feelings Before Doing This Step
Stuck, Alone, Lost, Confused, Afraid

Feelings After Doing This Step
Found, Graceful, Purposeful, Hopeful

Associations with This Step

Stone – Amethyst *(opening)*
Animals – Owl, Tiger, Phoenix, Hawk, Hummingbird
Fictional/Nonfictional Characters – Martin Luther King Jr., Oprah
Fairy Tales – *Cinderella, Sleeping Beauty*
Songs – "Climb Every Mountain" (Sound of Music), "I Will Survive" (Gloria Gaynor)
Images – Thriver Hero's Journey

SAMPLE WRITING from Tawanda, *a Thriver Success Story in Part Four of this book.*

I love the story of *Moana* (a Disney animated movie) because... Moana had a dream and vision for her life. She didn't allow anyone to stand in her way. As a youngster, she had no choice but to follow her parent's journey. As she grew, she followed her own heart and accomplished her goals. She became the leader of her family and broke traditions.

Lessons I've learned from it are: Never give up on your dreams; you can follow someone and like their way of doing things, but you won't find joy until you fulfill your own quest. Stand up for what you think is right. Believe in yourself. It's okay to take risks. Your family's beliefs and lessons will always be with you and will guide you, but you must walk your own path.

– Tawanda

STEP 2: QUIET INNER CRITIC

Feelings Before Doing This Step

Crazy, Overwhelmed, Self-Doubt, Defeated Down, Disorganized, Angry, Failure, Nothing, Depressed, Judged

Feelings After Doing This Step

Organized, Joyful, Stronger, Hopeful, Up, Deserving, Freedom, Refreshed, Tranquil, Relieved, Competent, Moving Forward, Unstuck, Soothed

Associations with This Step

Stone – Sodalite *(order, calmness, truth)*
Animals – Elephant, Alligator, Hyena, Bear, Spider
Fictional/Nonfictional Characters – Bert/Ernie
Fairy Tales – *Jack and the Bean Stalk* (the killing of the giant)
Stories – *Slay the Dragon, Mean Girls*
Songs – "Breakaway" (Kelly Clarkston)
Images – View of a Vista at the Top of a Mountain

<u>SAMPLE WRITING</u> *from Cathryn, a Thriver Success Story in Part Four of this book*

So many negative voices had gotten inside my head, telling me that I am worthless, so I have to be active in countering these negative thoughts. So I use the exercise Susan does with us on this step in her workshops in my daily life. When a negative thought comes up, I write it down on a piece of paper. Then I draw a line down the center of the page and on the other side of that line, I write the truth in the most positive way I can. Countering that negative thought with my truth allows me to let go of the negativity and visualize the positive. I have progressed tremendously in this process of quieting my Inner Critic.

At first, to stop the negative thought in my head, I had to write down both the negative and positive. Now I don't write anything down. I recognize a thought as negative, counter it with the truth in my head and move on. Shortcutting that process shows where I am today as a thriver. My truth is much more solid, like a wall, and a negative thought doesn't even enter my space. When people say negative things to me, I think,

Okay, that's about them. They are having a bad day. That's not about me. Sometimes a negative thought can even be disguised in a genuinely caring way, such as "I care about you. That's why I'm trying to help you figure out your life better." In other words, they are saying that I need to be fixed. But I tell myself, "Forget about it. They don't know my life."

– Cathryn

SAMPLE WRITING *from Adrienne, a Thriver Success Story in Part Four of this book*

As I am packing up my house to sell it and move to North Carolina, fear creeps in like a breeze. It turns into a cold wind biting my face. I am feeling helpless; I can't do this alone. I keep finding pictures of my parents, my dad and my brother. ALL GONE – I AM SO ALONE. Skin tingling. Tears. So many triggers.

I speak out loud to myself, "Adrienne, you need to settle down." Nothing.

I repeat, "Adrienne, if you can relax just a little, you can breathe again."

I get up. I pace, looking at piles of stuff all around. My mom's glassware, my daughter's memories from high school. All of a sudden, a crack in the anxiety-ridden prison of my mind.

"Wait, Adrienne! You are a Thriver!"

I get a poster board and start writing affirmations. I write:

- I will thrive through this great change.
- I am courageous.
- I can breathe.
- I am doing this.
- I am okay.
- I am fine.

I breathe in slowly and deeply. I exhale. I have come down from a 10 to a 5 on an anxiety scale of 1 to 10. I think of things I learned from Susan. Remember a time you overcame a great obstacle. My memories go back to the beginning of my divorce. I felt as if I were coming out of my skin. Desperate like a wild animal. Am I going to play dead? No, I realize that the constricted feeling of my being is not be feared.

I remember that our Thriver image is a butterfly. Out of the chrysalis comes a beautiful butterfly with wings to navigate the world. How can we thrive if we don't realize and embrace the moment when we shed our skin? We must be like a snake shedding its skin in order to grow.

We must blast through the constriction of our eminent growth to the chrysalis.
My inner child says, "Let's do it! *Wheeeeeeee!*"
I tell myself that I need patience. I choose to live happy. This is how I thrive.
Awareness is the first step to change.
Thank you, Susan!

– **Adrienne**

STEP 3: CONNECT WITH THE HAPPY PERSON INSIDE YOU

Feelings Before Doing This Step

Low Energy, Lonely, Deprived, Foreign,

Feelings After Doing This Step

Energetic, Connected, Loved, Full of Purpose, Joy, Glowing, Celebration, Power Is Turned On, Part of the Circle, Protected, Inspired

Associations with This Step

Stone – Rose Quartz *(universal love)*
Animals – Cat, Dog, Laughing Hyena, Bunny, Dolphin
Fictional/Nonfictional Characters – Ernie *(Sesame Street)*, Tigger, Maya Angelou
Fairy Tales – *Cinderella* (talking to the animals)
Songs – "Happy" (Pharrell), "Part of Me" (Katy Perry), "She's a Butterfly" (Martina McBride)
Images – Beach, Sunset, Build a Fire, Northern Star

Living in the Thriver Zone

SAMPLE WRITING: *Letter to Donna from her Happy Person Inside*

Dear Donna,

I am the Happy Person Inside. I want to tell you something.

You can shake off those fears, those dark, scary, depressive thoughts. Those thoughts are not from God. You, my dear, are a strong, loving, kind and passionate person. Believe in yourself! You are such a joyous soul, only inches away at any moment from placing a random smile across your face and doing a dance step across the room. Your days of believing that other humans can speak your truth are over. You feel in your being that their harsh words, names and accusations thrown at you cannot diminish your power but only show their own insecurities.

Now, take a deep breath; raise your head up, chin high, and wipe away those tears. Feel how blessed you are for every experience on your journey. Break open the cocoon, for it is time to FLY! Shine brightly and speak truth into the darkness in the world.

BE CHANGE
BE LIGHT
BE TRUTH
BE STRONG
BE HELP
And sometimes, BE HELPED!

Love you,

The Happy, Serene, Faithful, Being Inside (AKA Your Soul)

– Donna

SAMPLE WRITING: *Letter to Suzanne from her Happy Person Inside*

Dear Suzanne:

I'm the Happy Person Inside and I want to tell you something…

You are MAGNIFICENT! I love you. I adore you. I celebrate and support you!

You don't talk to me – AT ALL – EVER. We need to talk ALL THE TIME! You doubt yourself, and that is WRONG. You don't trust yourself and THAT is wrong. You encourage other women to love and support themselves but then you don't encourage YOU!

It's OK. You've simply developed habits over a lifetime that you needed in order to SURVIVE. But now that's all you do <u>is</u> SURVIVE. There is a big, bold, MAGNIFICENT life that is ready for you and all you need to do (<u>really</u>, ALL you need to do) is say <u>YES</u> and step into it.

Please, Suzanne, say <u>YES</u>. You don't need help. You don't need assistance. (Of course, you HAVE love and support if you need to reach out.) I want you to have the confidence to step into YOU and BE HER already. It's OK to fail, but you <u>WON'T</u>. You will <u>SUCCEED</u>. It is your <u>TIME</u>. You can celebrate Suzanne. And <u>no one</u> can take that away from you. No one will ever take anything away from you AGAIN. Not ever. No more loss. No more struggle. No more pain only JOY!!! Only CELEBRATION!!! Only HOORAY!!! You <u>DO</u> deserve. You are a <u>SUCCESS</u>. Please believe me, Suzanne. You know it's true. Let the truth <u>SHINE</u>.

– Suzanne

<u>SAMPLE WRITING</u> *from Teri on the Happy Person Inside You*

Susan's work introduced me to a space untouched by the abuse I have experienced. There my Happy Person Inside and I walk hand-in-hand as I rise from survivor to thriver!

With all growth, there are many challenges along the way. For me the thought-provoking, soul-searching work and encouragement that Susan has provided to me made those challenges easier to move through.

The world through the eyes of a thriver is an exciting view, and I am thankful for the work that got me here. The exercise of writing a letter to my Happy Person Inside introduced me to a part of me that I never imagined existed. I knew myself as a victim, worked hard to get to know myself as a survivor and that is where I thought abused people lived. But Susan's work showed me that there was so much more. There is this untouched space in all of us that is just waiting to be discovered.

– Teri

STEP 4: GET POSITIVE ENERGY

Feelings Before Doing This Step
Sad, Alone, Heavyhearted, Anxious, Drained, Depressed, Seeking Refuge, Dark Mood, Black Cloud, Confused

Feelings After Doing This Step
Joy, Connected, Lighthearted, Peaceful, Energetic, Content, Grateful, Loved

Associations with This Step

Stone – Carnelian *(vitality, positive life choices)*
Animals – Butterfly, Gecko, Chameleon, Lamb, Cardinal, Robin
Fictional/Nonfictional Characters – Oprah, Sophia, Lundy Bancroft
Fairy Tales – *Snow White and Seven Dwarfs* (especially "Happy")
Songs – "Fight Song" (Rachel Platten) "Let It Go," (from Frozen 1) "Part of Me" (Katy Perry), "She's a Butterfly" (Martina McBride)
Images – Thriver Friends, Memory of the Beach, Fall-to-Winter Season, Sunrise, Phoenix Rising

---

SAMPLE WRITING *from Leslie on Getting Positive Energy*

My Homework: Do something that makes you happy and write about it

Before – I can't do it. Don't know what to write about. Why is she making us do this? This sucks!

During – Okay, relax. You got this. You can do it.

After – That wasn't so bad. I did it. I feel HAPPY!

What makes me happy? Shopping with friends, with new friends, being with a new friend Before – I don't know, what if we don't get along, what if I get lost, what if she hates me, what if I hate her?

During – OMG! This is way more fun than shopping alone. You get feedback from a friend. You get to talk about anything and everything. I love this!

After – OMG! This was great! What was I so worried about? Was it the shopping or the new friend or both that was so great? I believe it was both. You need both. Things are better shared, and it sure is fun to have someone to talk to. It is time to take risks and make new friends. It is not the destination but the journey that you are on and who you meet. We can help each other along the way.

An Affirmation – I will seek out new friends, and we will help each other on this journey to find our Happy Ending.

– Leslie

STEP 5: VISION A NEW LIFE

Feelings Before Doing This Step
Powerless, Stuck, Status Quo, Incomplete, Unloved

Feelings After Doing This Step
Possibilities, Fulfillment, Abundance, Gratitude, Love, Openness, Freedom, Soaring, Flying, Dreams

Associations with This Step

Stone – Citrine *(energizes, imparts joy, wonder and delight)*
Animals – Eagle, Beaver
Fictional/Nonfictional Characters – Susan B. Anthony, Ella Grasso, Martin Luther King, Susan Omilian, Hillary Clinton, Malala Yousafzai
Fairy Tales/Stories – *The Little Engine That Could*
Songs – "We Are Family" (Sister Sledge), "I Have a Dream" (Abba)
Images – Caterpillar into Butterfly, Planting/Sprouting Seeds, First Crocus in Spring, Spread My Wings

SAMPLE WRITING *from Tawanda, The Happy Person Inside in the Future*

Our house! Yes, yes, yes! I finally did it. We are at our new house. The moving truck is outside, still full, but ready to be unpacked. My children are in a minor-shock stance. They are taking it all in. I'm excited – a little sad but mostly excited. The children are picking out their rooms as I unload the truck. Happy tears are forming in my eyes just by how happy my children are right now. We have bought a house with four bedrooms and two baths, all on one level. We have a basement that's finished and will be our extended living room and playroom. We have a garage, a deck and an enclosed indoor pool area. The boys have a basketball court outside, and my daughter has a custom-made doll house that she can play with inside. She loves it! We are blessed.

All of our hard work to get this house has paid off. It was hard for us to sacrifice going to events and buying extra things so we could save money for our house. And all the time it has taken to find and buy the house has been worth it. There is a different feeling when you own something for yourself. You tend to take better care of it. Now that everyone has their own room and space, I can't wait to watch my children explore things and use their imaginations to build their space to their liking. We stop unloading the truck now just to take our first selfie of us and our new house. Could you imagine that people doubted me about the house? That I could not do it or that I was beneath them? No, no, no, I deserve to be settled with a fresh start, owning my own home.

Now it's time to look at how we will decorate the house. We'll brainstorm ideas, smart shop, color coordinate, all that fun jazz. Right now we're happy and satisfied with knowing we have this home, the deed to it and the keys. We'll worry about how to furnish it later.

Congratulations to us, the little engine that could!

– **Tawanda**

Part Three

STEP 6: OVERCOMING FEAR

Feelings Before Doing This Step
I Cannot Do This, Defeated, Afraid, Scared, Terrified, Horrified

Feelings After Doing This Step
I Can Do This, Empowered, Brave, Bold, Confident, Complete

Associations with This Step

Stone – Emerald *(lets go of negative, attracts positive energy, overcomes problems)*
Animals – Killer Whale, Lion, Spider, Kangaroo, Bear, Barracuda, Shark
Fictional/Nonfictional Characters – Eleanor Roosevelt, Rosa Parks, Mallala Yousafzai, Hillary Clinton, Winnie the Pooh
Fairy Tales/Stories – *The Little Engine That Could*
Songs – "I Will Survive" (Gloria Gaynor), "Brave" (Sara Bareilles) "Part of Me" (Katy Perry)
Images – Skydiving, Deep-End Diving

SAMPLE WRITING *from Donna, If I Had No Fear, I Would…*

If I had no fear, I would continue to keep this word fear in small letters to not give it any power. I would walk into my new historic house boldly, with confidence and a joy-filled heart thrilled with the possibilities.

Realistically, fear will be a part of my adventure. It will exist every day, and I should celebrate its sensation. "Fear feelings" validate that I am simply in the midst of transforming to a more serene existence. Fear proves that I am walking from my comfort zone of what I am familiar with to the end of a spiritual dock, getting ready to jump into the waters filled with dreams and adventures. Jumping into the waters with a surge of empowerment and peace, knowing I will be lifted up to float above the water. I will not sink!

– Donna

STEP 7: SET NEW GOALS

Feelings Before Doing This Step
Unsure, Lethargic, Impossible, Stuck, Crazy, Disorganized, Self-Abasement, Unworthy

Feelings After Doing This Step
Focused, Motivated, Positive, Hopeful, Purposeful, Accomplished, Wow!

Associations with This Step

Stone – Goldstone *(ambition, courage, confidence, uplifting)*
Animals – Beaver, Ants, Bees, Birds
Fictional/Nonfictional Characters – Mother Teresa, Lundy Bancroft, Susan Omilian
Songs – "Unwritten" (Natasha Bedingfield), "Somewhere Over the Rainbow" (Wizard of Oz), "I Want to Live" (John Denver)
Images – Graduation

What would it feel like if we could take back our lives?

Joy, $$$, Kids, Time, Mind, Hope, Calm, Voice, Peace, Power, Bodies, Future, Respect, Hobbies, Dreams, Self-love, Interests, Strength, Fight in Me, Self-esteem, Independence, Success

---

GOAL: Move to a House on the Beach

- Sit in my home overlooking the ocean
- Move to the house
- Pack up my old house
- Buy the house on the beach
- Get financing for house — Fear: Is my credit good enough?
- Pick out house
- Vision the house
- Talk to a financial planner

This Week: Research and find a financial planner who can help me with a plan.

Overcoming Fear: Go on Internet to get free credit report and check my credit.

Part Three

HOW THE SEVEN STEPS WORK TOGETHER

The *Seven Steps to Thriving After Abuse* can also be seen as a whole, flowing together as you move through them, going forward toward fulfilling a desire. Below is a piece I wrote one day when I realized, to my surprise, how the Seven Steps to Thriving can move from one to the other and work seamlessly to reach a particular goal.

THE ACCIDENT:

On a Sunday evening in May, I was driving home from a weekend retreat I had conducted for about twenty women in the follow-up group of the *My Avenging Angel Workshops*™ program. We had spent the weekend together in a gorgeous beach house on the Connecticut shore reviewing and reflecting on the *Seven Steps to Thriving After Abuse* that are the centerpiece of my first book, *Entering the Thriver Zone*.

That Sunday night I was tired, exhausted by all the fun and activities of this amazing weekend with the women. Then too, I had packed my small compact car to the gills with all that I had brought to make the weekend retreat so special. As I was coming up from the shoreline toward the central part of the state, I drove off the road reaching to get something had fallen off the passenger seat onto my foot near the gas pedal. I smashed my car into the guard rail going about sixty-five miles an hour.

BOOM! I didn't feel the car's impact against the rail as much as shock of the air bag burning into my chest. It saved me from going through the windshield, but it hurt! I got out of the car in one piece, but in shock. I couldn't believe what I had done to my car – it was totaled – and I didn't know how I was going to get myself and my damaged- beyond-repair car home.

THE MIRACLE:

It was a miracle for sure that I was there, alive and all right, but the real miracle came in dealing with the aftermath of it all. From the moment the car stopped, my Inner Critic, the negative voice in my head, began screaming at me.

You should have been paying more attention. You shouldn't have loaded the car like that with stuff piled on the passenger seat. What are you going to do for a car? How are you going to get home? You had such a great time over the weekend, and now you spoiled it! How are you going to deal with all this?

As that voice went on, fortunately people stopped to help me there on the side of the highway. They called 911 for me and waited with me until the police and tow truck showed up. When my car was towed to my house, I got help to remove what I needed from the car, and I watched it be towed away. Suddenly I was home in my house, yes, grateful to be alive, but overwhelmed and worried. I had no car, no transportation to get to work on Monday morning or any other place. What was I going to do? How was I going to fix this? Then I thought about the material we had gone over at the retreat – the *Seven Steps to Thriving After Abuse. Do they really work? Could they help me now? God knows, I needed some help! I'll give it a try.*

THE SEVEN STEPS!

What about those Seven Steps to Thriving? I claim they work after experiencing abuse; surely they could help with the aftermath of a car accident.

Quickly I went through them in my head step-by-step:

Step 1 – See the Journey that I am on from victim to survivor to thriver! *I can do more than just survive this car accident. In fact, I'm going to thrive after it. I know I can!*

Step 2 – Quiet the Inner Critic *It's loud and still yelling at me about how I could have avoided this accident and didn't. But that's over now. I can't change what has happened to me. I need to move on!*

Step 3 – Connect with the Happy Person Inside You *My car is totaled...but...I'M GOING TO GET A NEW CAR! YES! I've wanted one for a while and now I'll have one!*

Step 4 – Get Positive Energy *I am grateful I am still alive. I have so much more to accomplish in life, so many other women to help. I can do this!*

Step 5 – Vision a New Life *I could see myself in my new car, driving it, enjoying it and feeling energized about my life, my work. This happened for a reason. Embrace it!*

Step 6 – Overcome Your Fears that you don't know what to do next. *Yes, yes, I do know, and I can do it. I'll reach out and handle what I need to do – make an insurance claim, get a rental car and go to the dealership for a new car. I can do this. I need a plan. Help!*

Step 7 – Set New Goals *I have a plan! Call insurance company, rent a car, contact car dealership, negotiate deal, drive out with new car. Full of confidence, I go forward!*

Less than a week later...*I did it all! I now have a new car, and I checked out physically, so all is well. I am good and what I've learned is that you need to work all Seven Steps together. Although any one can be helpful, together they are amazing!*

THE SEVEN STEPS WORK!

I proved with my story that all things, including a car accident, happen for a reason! I now have a great example of how the Seven Steps work in my own life, and I want to include it in this book *Living in the Thriver Zone: A Celebration of Living Well as the Best Revenge*. It seems so appropriate!

AMAZING!

SECOND TOOL: MANIFESTING A LIFE OF POWER AND PURPOSE!

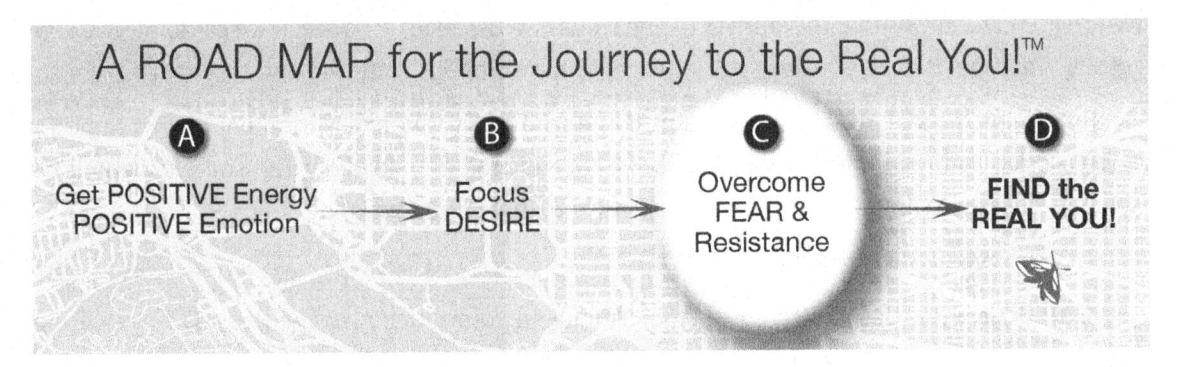

A ROAD MAP for the Journey to the Real You!™

A Get POSITIVE Energy POSITIVE Emotion → **B** Focus DESIRE → **C** Overcome FEAR & Resistance → **D** FIND the REAL YOU!

That which we manifest is before us:
We are the creators of our own destiny.

— GARTH STEIN

The Road Map for the Journey to the Real YOU™ is another part of the motivational model that I have used successfully with women who have experienced violence and abuse as well as keeping my own life moving forward. With this model, I have been able not merely to survive all the difficult things that have happened to me, including the violent and tragic death of my niece Maggie, but I have also moved on to thrive and find a life of purpose helping others!

Only in putting together this Road Map as part of my motivational model did I realize I had been using this process all of my life. But I only became aware of how natural it was while coping with an overwhelming loss in my life. In fact, with the unique and innovative work I now do with women who have been abused in light of what happened to Maggie, I have been able to:

- *discover opportunity in what I had considered only as a loss*
- *find positive energy to push myself forward*

Living in the Thriver Zone

- *dare to create the life I want*
- *overcome my fears to find the dynamic Real YOU inside*

What's great for me about this Road Map is that whenever I feel like I've lost my way, I get out my map and see where I am stuck. Maybe I have to slow down a little or avoid a detour so I can get back to manifesting my desires and finding the Real YOU, my authentic self. Over time, I have gone from only contacting my Real YOU for a few minutes each day to spending whole days, weeks, and even months in her wondrous company. In fact, what I have found is that connecting with our authentic selves is not that hard. It's just that when something really good happens to us, we think we are merely lucky or that the stars in the heavens have lined up for once. If we see someone else getting what she desires, we think she's special or has some "in" with the powers that be.

But the process of making our dreams come true every day, every moment is how the Universe works, and the sooner we learn how to use it more consciously, the sooner we will be living in the Real YOU – our Happy Ending! – every single moment of our lives.

So let's review the Road Map!

MAP POINT A – Get Positive Energy – You begin your journey to the Real YOU by inviting pure, positive energy into your life.

MAP POINT B – Focus Your Desires – Bring out your dreams and desires for a spin!

MAP POINT C – Overcome Your Fears – Push through your fears, limiting beliefs about yourself, knocking down the barriers to connecting with the Real YOU.

MAP POINT D – Find the Real YOU – Your Reward is to connect with the part of you untouched by all that has happened to you. Being there, you feel your Happy Ending!

Using this Map, you can manifest things you've dreamed of, never thought you'd be able to do.

PROMPT: Using the *Manifesting: A Fairy Tale* worksheet on the next page, write about something you thought you couldn't do and follow the prompts. You *can* make your dreams come true. If you've done it in the past, you can do it again!

See a SAMPLE WRITING from Margaux to show you how it's done! More writing samples for this exercise are in my book, *Staying in the Thriver Zone: A Road Map to Manifest a Life of Power and Purpose.*

There are so many amazing stories to tell in the Thriver Zone!

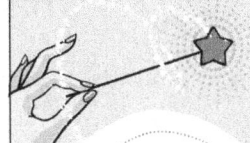

Manifesting– A Fairy Tale!

Make a list of things that you have done – big or small – that you thought you couldn't do, but you did! Pick one. Think of how you manifested that result. WRITE A STORY using prompts below. Have fun! Celebrate your success!

———————————

ONCE UPON A TIME there was a girl who thought she couldn't . . .

    She tried to…

    And then she tried…

    And she tried again…

There were negative voices in her head telling her…

But she decided not to listen. Instead positive voices told her…

In the end, she felt…(e.g., joy, strong, confident…)

She knew she felt her power when she…

Her experience taught her…the lessons learned…

With her success, she learned more about her purpose in life which is…

She knew she was living her HAPPILY EVER AFTER because…

MANIFESTING: A FAIRY TALE!
by Margaux

Once upon a time there was a girl who grew up thinking she couldn't be as smart or as loved as her two sisters because she was the adopted daughter. She never seemed to measure up. Growing up different in many ways and being treated in both subtle and not so subtle ways differently than her sisters contributed to her sense of diminished self-worth. Her struggle in not feeling valued or loved impacted her future relationships as well as diminished her belief that she was good enough or capable enough to succeed. This self-doubt ran deep and affected her in school, in her work and in her relationships with men.

She tried to find love in all the wrong places and struggled to find a place where she felt she belonged. For so long her attempts were ill-fated and even destructive to her life. She was going about it all wrong. She got married twice to men who were mean and abusive, but she realized after some time that her own mom had taught her to be the peacemaker no matter what. She knew that once she began to acknowledge these things, she could change them. She did not need to be the peacemaker with these husbands. They were mean, and she deserved better.

She tried to divorce her [second] husband twice, but he sabotaged every attempt for years until she finally moved into another house with her children. As soon as she got away, she went back to school and earned a degree – something she had always dreamed of. This was a huge step because although she never felt she was smart enough, now she was going for her master's degree. She knew she wanted to prove to herself and everyone in her past that she was capable and smart. Most of all, she wanted to be a great example for her children. She wanted them to see her work hard at something difficult and succeed. She wanted them to understand that it is never too late to change your path and improve your life. She wanted to show them what love was really about. Love comes from loving yourself first and then paying it forward.

The inner demons and critical voices in her head were fierce. She could hear her father telling her that he didn't believe it when she was tested in college several years earlier and had an impressive IQ score. She heard her husband telling her she could not afford to divorce him and all the horrible names he had called her through the years. She relived the stories of her adoption, and she was suffocated by feelings of not fitting in or belonging. She felt like an island – a very small and insignificant island.

The fear of trying and failing were intense and very real. She battled with herself to stay the course and not just quit and curl up in a ball and surrender. It was so scary for her to leave her marital home, to file for divorce and to go back to school. All of these events were scary and overwhelming enough individually, but as they were all happening at the same time, it was almost unbearable.

She decided not to listen to the negative voices and influences. She had to learn to cope and stay the course. She realized that she had to focus on each day to survive. She looked for what she had control of and could do THAT day to empower herself and to contribute to her future well-being. In doing this every day, she did not overwhelm herself with too many "what-ifs" and unknown future outcomes that she couldn't control.

Instead, she listened to other positive voices. She surrounded herself at school with positive thinkers and idea builders. She networked and earned the respect of her professors. She found study partners, future friends and many resources to help get her through. Later she called this process "building her team." She learned that for all the things you don't know or are not strong or good at, there are those who are, and they can help you. Asking for help is not a weakness, but rather it is a strength that positions you in life to get ahead. It is empowering and brave. She began to slowly believe that she was smart, that she was beautiful and well-liked.

She even found that others were seeking her help, advice and friendship. She graduated with a 4.2 GPA for her master's degree, and she found a great guy to date.

She knew she felt her power when she finally divorced her husband, moved to Florida with her fiancé and had the courage to start her own business there. Once again, she formed her team in her new home state. She has her lawyer, her CPA, her business mentors, and she has supportive, positive friends in place. She fully acknowledged that she didn't know everything she needed to know to start this business, but that was okay; her team would help her. This experience taught her that everyone has self-doubt and feelings of inadequacy at first, but it is okay and even normal to have these feelings. Feel them! But then understand and embrace that fear and find the resources and people to help you to reach your goals and obtain your dreams. Focus on what you can do today.

Because of her success, she knows that she is meant to help others overcome life challenges. Even her new business is helping others. She hopes she will continue to do so in many capacities for the rest of her life.

She knows she is living her HAPPILIY EVER AFTER because she is free of abusive relationships today. She is no longer held prisoner to her own inner critical voices and fears. She accepts the fear and negative voices as a part of her human state. She ventures out to challenge herself in any way she can with her team at her side. She looks to her future now as one big, fun adventure. There is nothing and no one in her way. She has love, support and help all around her. She breathes freely and sleeps well for the first time in her life. She is excited every morning to start the next day's adventure with the man she loves and the friends and supportive team she has around her. She is finally truly in charge of her life. There is no better way to feel. There is no better success than this. This is thriving!

– Margaux

With *The Seven Steps to Thriving After Abuse* and *A Road Map to Manifest a Life of Power and Purpose,* you now have tools to put into your toolbox for the journey from victim to survivor to thriver! The next part of this book will give you a chance to see how the seven women who are our Thriver Success Stories have used these tools to take their journey beyond abuse to living well. They will be your role models.

They are working on living the life of their dreams every day! You can too!

~ ~ ~ ~ ~ ~ ~ ~ ~ ~ ~ ~ ~

Happy ever after isn't a fairy tale.
It's a choice.
— FAWN WEAVER

*It is good to have

an end to journey toward;

but it is the journey

that matters in the end*

— Ursula K. LeGuin

Part Four

Thriver Success Stories

MEET THE SUPER HERO THRIVERS

*No one saves us but ourselves. No one can. No one may.
We ourselves must walk the path.*

— BUDDHA

I am a SUPER Hero THRIVER!

I have been so privileged and honored to have met and worked with so many wonderful women who have inspired me on their journey from victim to survivor to thriver. I want to celebrate their accomplishments, and I'm so impressed with their progress. In Part Four of this book, you'll get to read their stories in full and be as amazed as I am. We are thrivers!

At the end of this section, I have included the list of questions that I asked each of these women in their interviews so you can see the range of topics we discussed about their journeys to thriving. Before you do that, I wanted to highlight and summarize a few of these topics that were touched upon by each of women in their stories that I found particularly significant. I hope you can appreciate how articulate they were, as well as open and honest in sharing their journeys. And they were thrilled that their progress to thriving is acknowledged in this book!

I am so blessed to have found this work and gotten to know these women and so many others in our Thriver Community. I wish I had the time to interview them all and document their journeys in this book. But these seven women will stand in for all and be cheered!

Two of the topics in the interview are very dear to me. First, as I have stated in many places at many times, the idea that "living well is the best revenge" was the one thought that rescued me in the shock and sadness of my niece Maggie's murder in 1999 by her ex-boyfriend. Finding that quote from George Herbert when I googled "revenge" was lifesaving for me. I felt that because her ex-boyfriend had killed her and then himself, there was no revenge I could exact upon him on this earth. But I slowly found that my revenge would be the *My Avenging Angel Workshops*™ that I have conducted for the last twenty years for women helping them move on as Maggie could not. I am thrilled that this idea of "living well as the best revenge" has also captured the minds and hearts of these seven women and many more in our Thriver Community.

Second, I am also pleased that the women I have interviewed have found great value and worth in the community of women I have built through my workshop program. But I have to add that this Thriver Community has sustained me, too, over the years. The friendships I have made have been wonderful and I have had the chance to watch the women's children grow and be a witness to their own lives transforming. It doesn't get much better than this!

I want to thank all the women in this community and beyond to all of our supporters –financial and otherwise – who have kept the workshops, follow-up groups and retreat weekends I provide to the women in Connecticut free of charge. This is not a luxury item for the women! Thanks to all of the readers of my books and participants in my trainings. We are on an important mission – spreading the word that there is a journey beyond abuse to thriving!

Here's a summary of how these seven women described their journey from victim to survivor to thriver in each of the most common topics in our interviews.

SUMMARY FROM THE THRIVER SUCCESS STORIES

TOPIC #1 – LIVING WELL IS THE BEST REVENGE

ADRIENNE

Today, I am living well, and that has been my best revenge! My living well is that I wake up in the morning, feeling happy and grateful for everything that I have. Being positive now is just my way of being. Living well for me is also realizing that I am safe and secure, whole and complete just as I am. It took a long time for this kind of positive thinking to seep into my soul. The more I show gratitude and grace, the more I receive. Now that I am able to bring positive energy into my life every day, I feel so different. I realize that if what you do, think and say makes you feel good, you can create positive energy in your own soul.

CATHRYN

While I like the quote "living well is the best revenge," I like to focus on living well, not on revenge. My goal is to model for others what living well is, even for those in my life who have hurt me. I don't want them to stay stuck there, and I don't want to be angry at them. I want them to see that living well means taking control of your life. You are not in control of yourself when you are trying to control others.

I have this vision: There is an ocean, and I am a dolphin out in the ocean, just totally free. At the beginning of my journey, I was not free. I was in a net. Now I am out in the ocean, swimming without constraints. I can go anywhere I want and do whatever I want because I am free. There is nobody forcing me out of fear, or control or whatever to do what they say I have to do. I can choose to do whatever I want to.

Being the dolphin in this situation makes me feel like no one can hold power over me anymore because I know who I am, God loves me and I have a purpose.

JENNY

The quote "living well is best revenge" is the starting point of the journey after abuse because you'll eventually get to a place where you don't need to avenge the abuse anymore. Eventually you see that the abuse was something that happened to you, and you learn from it and then go on with your life. Not that what happened to me doesn't still affect me. There are times during the year that catch me off guard. I find myself being irritable and wound up, and I remember that I'm in that part of the year when it got really tumultuous for me and my body still reacts to this day. But within the past year, I'm at the point that I don't hope anything bad happens anymore to my ex-husband who was abusive to me. I'm over the karma thing. Hurt people hurt people. I'm not in a place where I'm hurting anymore. I hope he got help and that he's in a better place, and I hope he is a better person.

I am amazed at how far I have come after meeting Susan almost ten years ago. I am grateful for the journey and where I am now. But her workshop only opens the door. You go to a workshop and someone opens that door and there is the path to a more fulfilling life. It's up to you to walk through and do the work. But then before you went to the workshop, maybe you couldn't find the door.

PAMELA
I am on the road to living well because now I'm focused on how I am living and what I want out of life. I can decide what kind of person I want to be, what I want to do and what kind of relationships I want to have. My biggest dream is to write books for children that would help them notice that something may not be right in their homes. When they do figure it out, then they can offhandedly say something to a friend or a teacher or an adult without it being really obvious and get the help they need.

I'd like to do picture books with different characters with each book dealing with an issue. The book would tell the kids what shouldn't happen in their homes or at school. I have already written a story about a girl with low self-esteem who gets bullied.

My vision for my life today is to take the talents and skills I have and combine them into a career – a business that can help children or adults by showing them how they can make a change in their lives. I'd like to be a working artist, creating books for children and working every day, like in a painting workshop. This would make me happy and bring me great joy.

Part Four

SOPHIA

For me, living well is about living in a place of peace and joy. There I can I think about what I want my life to look like, and I know that I can manifest all those desires if I stay with positive thoughts and push through my fears. That's the motivational model that Susan teaches and that matches my own life experiences. When I am living well, I don't question whether I am good enough or who am I to dream of a better life.

Living well as the best revenge is not about the people who have hurt you. It was never about them for me. It is about my health and my knowing that I do not want abuse in my relationships. Yet my own adversity has helped me champion so many women who need to assess or come out of potentially abusive relationships. If I was a role model for them, they might have thought that my relationship looked good from the outside. But it was plagued with domestic violence, and I was able to terminate that relationship, which was the right thing for me to do. Today my living well allows others to see that if they have the self-determination and the courage to be triumphant, they, too, can leave an abusive relationship and move forward to find the life of their dreams.

TAWANDA

Living well feels like now I'm doing things that I thought I'd never be able to do or that I couldn't do. When I first came to the workshops, I wasn't able to get a job, and I wasn't convinced that I could get one. Going to the workshops helped me not only quiet the Inner Critic about those doubts, but also enabled me to go through weight-loss surgery. I would never have been able to do that without knowing that I could live beyond all my challenges and have a better life.

I feel good about being in the Thriver Zone. It was difficult for me to step out of just surviving – my Comfort Zone – into the Thriver Zone. I still have some fear that I may fall back into that survivor place, but I know I can keep on thriving. I can do it! I feel very powerful at times, and I have lots of purpose. I'm in the game of changing people's lives. So many people have been in my corner and helped me change mine. My way of giving back is being there to help support others and lead them in the right direction.

TENNILLE

I love when Susan tells us that living well is the best revenge. To me, living well means not hanging on to any of my bitterness. As a thriver, I've learned to process and react to things differently. Not everything needs to be argued or needs a response. Absolutely not! In fact, I'm not going to entertain thoughts like that or spend sleepless nights worrying about them. I've learned that when everything moves along smoothly, there is so much less anxiety in my life, and I can stay more focused on the important things, like living well and accomplishing my goals.

When I see how the other women in Susan's Thriver Community are living well, I can feed off of their positive energy. We bring each other up and give each other the courage to move forward with our lives. I never have had to say, "Oh, that woman still looks miserable." Everyone in the group is happy when we are together! We have a wonderful time! Susan's work has been life-changing for all of us.

TOPIC #2 – MOST HELPFUL STEPS

ADRIENNE

What I learned from Susan is that to get to thriving, I had to get positive energy into my life. Every step of Susan's *Seven Steps to Thriving After Abuse* helped me to do that. The *First Step: See the Journey* helped me see where I wanted to go and that I wanted to be a thriver. The *Second Step: Quiet the Inner Critic* became so important to me because I didn't know that the voice inside me that constantly criticized me and put me down was my Inner Critic. I also learned that the Inner Critic was only one of the voices in my head and that I could drown the Inner Critic by using the *Third Step: Connect with the Happy Person Inside You.* That is the part of me untouched by anything that had ever happened, and it brought me to *Step Four: Get Positive Energy* and *Step Five: Vision a New Life*. With those positive thoughts and emotions, I could vision a new future for myself with unlimited possibilities. What a thought! Learning how to use all these steps together was a healing moment for me.

Then, with *Step Six: Overcome Fears,* I was able to see that the limiting beliefs about myself were connected to the Inner Critic and when they came up as fears, I could combat them with positive affirmations. That way even little fears wouldn't turn into big ones and, in fact, Susan helped me see that I already had a positive pattern of overcoming fear in the past. I could use that pattern to confront my present-day fears and work toward the vision I have for a better, more positive future. Finally, in *Step Seven: Set New Goals*, Susan's suggestion that we start from the last thing we'd need to do to accomplish our goal down to the first gave me the confidence that I could achieve my goals step-by-step.

CATHRYN

Back when I was feeling powerless from the abuse I had experienced, I did not see a future for myself of fulfilling adventures. But once I realized in Susan's workshops that I was on a journey that could take me beyond just surviving, I felt I could take my power back, get strong enough to live a great life and even help others. The exercise Susan had us do in *Step Five, Vision a New Life*, helped me set a vision to do exactly that.

Another exercise called *Step Four: Get Positive Energy* has also been helpful to me. I needed to learn the ways I get positive energy so I could build up my strength, overcome obstacles and challenges and not feel so powerless. I needed my power back, not power over anyone else, but my own power to enable me to live my life well. In this step, Susan had us write about what makes us happy and how we feel before, during and after we do it. If we haven't done it in a long time, then she suggests that we go do it and then write about it afterward.

I love hiking. I love being on the top of a mountain looking out and down on everything. That is the best! It really fills me up. I also like being out in nature in general as well as singing and listening to music that fills me with joy and energy. Realizing what makes me happy means I can now more easily take that journey from feeling down and discouraged to being mostly filled with joy all the time. That's where I am now. I go do something I love to do, such as hike a mountain or listen to music for two hours, and then I feel so much better. I find that if I'm down, I really need two hours hiking or being in nature. One hour doesn't seem to do it for me. Two hours listening to songs works for me. The first hour I may be barely singing the words, but by the end of the second hour, I'm totally filled with joy again.

JENNY

Reconnecting with my Happy Person Inside – *Step Three: Connect with the Happy Person Inside You* – who has such wisdom and encouragement for me, was very emotional.

I remember crying while I read my piece to the women in the workshop, but everyone was so supportive. Susan told me to see the tears as a release, and they were.

Another helpful exercise in Susan's workshop was in *Step Two: Quiet the Inner Critic*. I leaned how important it was for me to acknowledge that I had an inner negative voice and to identify where that voice was coming from. When you hear it, you wonder if it is your own internal dialogue. *Am I still running the loops on my ex or my mother's insecurities, having been raised by her? Is that voice really something that I am thinking or did I pick that up from someplace else? Is it really relevant to what's going in my life right now?*

I know that my Inner Critic feeds the fear that holds me back by replaying what I was told coming from my background as a child. There thoughts were instilled in me like "Don't try that! You could fail!" Or "If you aren't good at something, why continue to do it when you are so awful at it?" Why couldn't I just enjoy doing something even if I know I'm not good at but I really like doing it?

You carry on these negative thoughts that your parents probably got from their parents, and it's like one big, negative cycle from one generation to another. I can see how my mom, who lived in this very small world with a critical mother, could have developed a super loud Inner Critic that then was channeled into the rest of us. Now I'm breaking that cycle and letting go of other people's expectations as well as any fear that is holding me back. I have to lighten my load and not be weighed down by other people's stuff.

PAMELA

When Susan began her workshop with *Step One: See Your Journey* from her *Seven Steps to Thriving After Abuse,* I was asked to pick out a fairy tale to write about for the exercise. I immediately said Cinderella. I always felt a connection to her because of the animals and how she talked to them. But Susan helped me see how Cinderella transformed by the end of the story. Susan said that Cinderella found her happy ending with the prince by completing herself as a person first and then finding a complete person in the prince. Susan's telling of the story surprised me because I always thought of myself as a bad person and thought nothing good would ever happen to me. Susan talked about Cinderella's movement from struggle to transformation to happy ending as a journey.

When she wrote on the board VICTIM to SURVIVOR to THRIVER to describe the journey we were on as victims of domestic violence, I knew right then that my goal was to be a thriver. I did see myself then as a survivor, even although I was still in an abusive relationship, but Susan gave me the idea that there was something more I could focus on as a thriver. While the women in the workshop really impressed me with their visions for the future, I didn't have much to say about my future because I was still really inside myself and withdrawn. At that time I had this idea that when you are born, you pick who you are going to be and what kind of life you were going to have. I believed that I was put on this earth just to suffer and get through it.

When we did the exercise in *Step Two: Quiet the Inner Critic* of Susan's *Seven Steps to Thriving After Abuse,* I thought, *What am I telling myself? Was it my Inner Critic and not me that was saying all that negative stuff about me?* I knew everyone has a good side and a bad side, but because of my upbringing and the relationship I was in at the time, I thought everything about me was bad. Sure, I had to help people around me, but I would never have anything. I'd never get beyond the suffering. But Susan and the other women in the workshop challenged all that. I loved that the women were open and loving, with warm personalities. They were so comfortable in their skins, and that's something I wanted to have. I want to be authentic and find out who I really am.

SOPHIA

One of Susan's exercises that really helped me on my journey to thriving was creating my own *I Am a Woman of Power* statement. It started with:

> *I am a woman of power who has made a positive impact on the world*
> *through my own healing, wellness and creativity.*
> (See Sophia's full statement later in this book.)

That word, *power,* is profound to me. I have power, and I will not give my power away to anyone. I am not powerless. I am powerful.

Another helpful exercise to me was in *Step Three: Connect with the Happy Person Inside You.* Writing a letter to myself from the Happy Person Inside allowed me to reconnect with what makes me happy. Oftentimes we, particularly as women, are so busy making other people happy that we forget about what makes us happy. It can be so simple. For me, being happy is about peace. It is about joy. It is about protecting my power. Going to Susan's workshop made me realize that I had lost my power and I needed to get it back. But I didn't want the kind of power when someone takes control over another person. I'm talking about "shared" power in a relationship where I am able to do what I need to do and who I am is recognized and supported by my partner. Living a life that is empowering is what thriving is all about.

TAWANDA

With all Susan's encouragement in the workshop, I began to work with the *Seven Steps to Thriving After Abuse* to see if I could break through the obstacles in my life. It made sense to me that I was on a journey – victim to survivor to thriver – and I loved how the exercise for that, *Step One: See Your Journey,* worked for me. But because I had been living in the victim role for so long, it was harder for me to do the rest of the steps.

At first, the toughest one for me was *Step Three: Connect with the Happy Person Inside You.* To connect with a part of me that was happy and positive seemed impossible. As a mom with three young children and the oldest sibling in my family, I have always been counted on to take care of others and not myself. Also being in an abusive relationship at the time was destroying my self-concept, and I had sunken down into a dark place. I didn't believe I deserved to explore that Happy Person Inside, so why even bother to find out what she was about?

But I took the chance, and to my surprise there was, as Susan suggested, a part of me untouched by all that had ever happened to me. I thought that if I had a Happy Person Inside of me, she had just gone away because of all the negative vibes and tension in my life. But once I wrote the letter to me from the Happy Person Inside, Susan's writing prompt for Step Three, suddenly she was there! She was alive and wanted to be heard.

One step I would have like to have learned earlier on my journey was how to quiet the Inner Critic. If you hear something for so long, you start to believe it, and that's the worst feeling. It's bad enough if someone says it, but don't start believing it yourself. It will just get you down, and you'll never get up.

Part Four

TENNILLE

When I first came to Susan's workshop, I was feeling okay about myself. I wasn't thinking that a lot was wrong in my life until Susan did the exercise with us for *Step One: See Your Journey* of her *Seven Steps to Thriving After Abuse*. She wrote "VICTIM to SURVIVOR to THRIVER" on the board and talked about how the journey after being abused was from struggle to transformation to happy ending. It was then that I realized I wasn't living in my happy ending. In fact, I was somewhere in between victim and survivor, but I hadn't really put much thought into it.

At the time I was newly engaged and thinking, *I'm happy. This is great! I'm going to get married again.* But by the middle of the first session of the workshop, suddenly my victim mentality switched on in my brain and I thought, *This is not right. This is not how it is supposed to feel.* I wondered, *Am I in another abusive relationship?* This one wasn't physical, but something was not right about it.

Then, in the exercise for *Step Three: Connect with the Happy Person Inside You*, Susan had us write a letter to ourselves from our Happy Person Inside, and I got to thinking again – something was not right in my life. I need to fix it. I would have to dig really deep and see what it was bothering me and what was best for me. Maybe I still would marry my fiancé, but I had to figure this out.

In *Step Five: Vision a New Life,* Susan gave us an exercise where our Happy Person Inside was in the future. I wrote about seeing her running to get into shape and feeling better, more energized and more positive. That made me want to go home, start running with my Happy Person Inside You and write about how it felt before, during and after. I felt so good about running that Sunday morning, but instead of support, I got resistance from my fiancé. He asked me why I was doing this, saying that he didn't really understand. That was another "light bulb" going off in my head about the relationship. That's not very healthy. With the physical abuse in my previous relationship, the warning signs of danger were clearer to me, and so I left. But this time, I'd been saying to myself, *"He's not hitting me, so it's really not abuse."*

Suddenly something just clicked inside my head, and I felt a surge of empowerment. What if I married him and was miserable? I'd have to get divorced and getting out of a marriage later would be much more complicated than getting out of an engagement now. I could see that attending Susan's workshop would help me set a new vision for my life. Ending that relationship was a perfect opportunity for me to start over.

TOPIC #3 – THE THRIVER COMMUNITY

ADRIENNE

Susan's follow-up group for the women who complete her two-day workshop was also very important in helping me to keep my positive energy flowing. Since the women in this group, like me, have experienced some kind of abuse and now we are moving beyond it, we have a strong, common bond – stronger than family for me. When you are with others in Susan's Thriver Community, you get energy just from being in the same room. I have become a role model and mentor in the group, even though I don't want people to think I'm better than anyone else. I was thriving so much, accomplishing so many of my goals, that I needed to share my progress with other like-minded women in the group. The women wanted to know how I did it, and I needed their support and friendship.

CATHRYN

What has helped me most on my healing journey has been Susan's commitment to build a continuing Thriver Community for the women who attend her workshops. Susan offers a follow-up group for women who complete her two-day workshop. I have done other programs that were ten-week sessions from start and finish, and then you'd never see anyone again. I liked that there is a backup for you in Susan's program whenever you need it.

I don't always attend the monthly events or the annual weekend retreats, but knowing that they are there and getting the emails from Susan about them gives me a sense of being grounded. If I need this place, it is there, an enveloping cocoon of nonjudgmental support when things get difficult in my life. I love to go to the events whenever I can because it's so helpful for me to feel this sense of community and belonging with people whose lifestyle or culture might be totally different than mine, but there is a commonality of overcoming abuse. I feel a sense of acceptance there that I don't necessarily have anywhere else. There are other people who are really close to me in my life, but they don't get that part of my experience. If they have walked with me while I was on that part of my journey, they may understand what I've gone through pretty well, but still it's not the same as someone who has been through it.

Another thing I like about Susan's Thriver Community is that we don't spend time talking about our stories of abuse and violence. Susan makes sure that we are safe, and if we are in need of crisis intervention services at any time, she'll make a referral to a domestic violence or sexual assault intervention program or other resources that can help women on the first part of the journey from victim to survivor. Because of that, Susan's workshops and follow-up activities are an emotionally safe place for me. It is a supportive social group where I don't have to constantly explain myself; everyone there understands that sometimes we can be triggered back into a bad space, but we don't have to stay there. For me, once I had a place to be an emotionally safe, I could start imagining a life free from fear and free from being controlled. I could take control of my own life and make my own choices. For me, that was my journey out of abuse, through being a survivor and on to becoming a thriver and living well!

JENNY
I remember coming to the workshop and finding that there were women there who had come through abuse and had been in Susan's program for a while. I could see that they were in a different place in their lives, and I felt that here I could find a way out of this. Not only were they showing me that there was a way to get to a different place, but also hearing the other women talk, it was so clear to me that they did not bring this abuse upon themselves. This was not their fault. If you can accept that about someone else, it makes it a lot easier to accept it about yourself.

One of the first things I remember doing in Susan's workshop was decorating a journal while quiet music was playing. That was a nice way to step out of myself and into that place where I could be creative. It was a great way to start things, and it helped make the workshop a safe place to be emotionally, even though I still wasn't comfortable processing my experience there in that way. It wasn't safe for me for me to process it emotionally in front of my parents, and I didn't have a close network of friends at that time that I could lean on. But Susan's workshop and the writing we did there became the safe, supportive place where I could process what I was going through when I was ready.

PAMELA

When I came into Susan's workshop, I thought everything about me was bad. Sure, I had to help people around me, but I would never have anything. I'd never get beyond the suffering. But Susan and the other women in the workshop challenged all that. I loved that the women were open and loving, with warm personalities. They were so comfortable in their skins, and that's something I wanted to have. I want to be authentic and find out who I really am.

SOPHIA

In the workshop, Susan helped me answer the call and begin my journey from victim to survivor to thriver. I was sure that I no longer wanted domestic violence to be the norm in my life, and I knew that life was not a destination, but a journey. But I found the help I needed in Susan's Thriver Community to take that journey and move forward with my life. I had never heard about being a "thriver" before I met Susan, and with that new word, I knew it was the place where I wanted to be. Hearing the word thriver repeatedly in Susan's group embedded the idea in my mind and heart that being a thriver means you are moving forward and going places! I wanted to function and operate in a way that showed everyone around me what being a thriver looked like.

I have been inspired by the women in Susan's Thriver Community who have done amazing things! One woman has become the CEO of an organization, and another has turned her land into an organic farm, a goal she accomplished after attending Susan's workshop. She connected her passion for educating people on nutrition and healthy eating to that goal, and her dream became a reality with the positive energy and support of the Thriver Community. As Maya Angelou says, "We are at our best when we inspire, encourage and connect with another human being." I believe we are hardwired as humans to connect to each other so we are not on life's journey alone. I am at my greatest when I am connected to other women, and we bring forth each other's greatness.

TAWANDA

Coming into Susan's group, I was feeling like a low person, but with these women, I was a part of something bigger inside my sisterhood. There, people were happy to see me, and in my regular life at that time, people weren't too happy with me. To be around people who had that good, positive energy, knowing that I could move on like them and make it in the world, felt so good. With that energy, I got the idea that maybe I could make a brighter future for myself, even though there was so much sadness in me being in a toxic relationship and struggling with so much. I dreaded going home from our follow-up gatherings. I'd stay until the last thing was cleaned up.

Being in Susan's Thriver Community is the best thing that ever happened to me. I get joy out of all of the activities, but what has been most productive for me is repeating and coming back to the two-day workshop. Even though I'm in the Thriver Zone now, there is always something I can learn. I can dig deeper and keep myself out of that victim or even survivor place. I am reminded to keep going and not to push things to the side or cover them up.

Each time I go back through a workshop, I amaze myself! I get to writing, and I can't stop. I write about things I didn't even know were there inside me. In some of my writing journals from previous workshops, I found that there was definitely a difference in what I wrote from one workshop to another, sometimes even in the same year. There are usually similarities in what I write about the Happy Person Inside You and my vision for the future, but sometimes I write something different in *Step One: See Your Journey* and the fairy tale or children's story we write about there. But there are some awesome things that I have been saying to myself year after year as I get deeper and deeper into who the Happy Person Inside of me is, and now all that is coming out on the surface.

TENNILLE

Being a part of Susan's Thriver Community has been great! No judgment passed there, and I have connected with women who are role models for me. I can see their happiness and how talented they are with their writing or music or whatever! They are women who are not afraid to move forward with their lives, and they inspire me. If they can do it, I can do it too. I love the energy buzzing around them, and I want to be a part of it. They invite me to events or activities and give me words of support and encouragement. I love going to all our Thriver Community events where I am surrounded by all that positivity.

TOPIC #4 – A LIFE OF POWER AND PURPOSE

ADRIENNE

By living well, I have found a life of power and purpose as a thriver. The longer I live in the Thriver Zone, the more I am able to feel my power. Having been abused or suffering trauma in your life can make you a bit meek. You want to be empowered to take your live forward and see a new vision for yourself. This is not the kind of power over you or that can be used against you to control you and make you feel bad. Instead, you are empowered to change your life and the lives of others so that everyone has the opportunity to live well.

My purpose in life changes all the time. Right now, my purpose is to make myself happy. I've spent many, many years taking care of others, so now I want a calm place to live and to heal myself for my next act in life. I know that what's next is going to be big because I'm always going to dream big – bigger and bigger now that I am thriving! This is truly my best revenge, making bigger and bigger dreams come true each day!

CATHRYN

Susan's program helped me to see that after experiencing abuse and being revictimized by the systems around me, I still had value. I could have a good future and take my power back. Today, I am a woman of power. As a Christian, I get my power from Jesus Christ. Negative words from people cannot come between me and the love and value that I have from Him. That is definitely the Real Me.

Finding the Real Me has given me a purpose in life. I want to help victims of domestic violence take the journey beyond abuse so they can thrive as I have. One of the ways I have begun to fulfill this purpose is to work on completing my bachelor's degree in psychology. My studies in this field have helped me to shape the dreams and ideas I have for how to do this work.

JENNY

Having a life of power and purpose as a thriver is a lot of trial and error, but to find things that resonates with you, you have to be open and looking for them. That's harder when you are stuck in what society expects you to do. For example, I spent a lot of money on my education, and I have a really good career. People would consider me as being successful. But what if what you are doing no longer feels fulfilling? You have to ask yourself what kinds of things could make you feel excited. I know I get excited when I see my friend who is a photographer posting stuff about her business growing. I get excited when I'm listening to *The Same 24 Hours,* one of my favorite author's podcast. She went from a career as a really successful lawyer to now being a writer, hosting a podcast and coaching athletes. She is on a journey of self-discovery, and I feel like that's what I should be doing now in my life. I should be discovering who I want to be, what I want to do and how I can work to get there.

PAMELA

My vision for my life today is to take the talents and skills I have and combine them into a career – a business that can help children or adults by showing them how they can make changes in their lives. I'd like to be a working artist, creating books for children and working every day, like in a painting workshop This would make me happy and bring me great joy.

SOPHIA

For me living a life of power and purpose as a thriver is an ongoing process. Although we are always evolving and changing like the butterfly, it is clear that without violence clouding our lives, we are more able to see life's purpose. I believe that God has given us all a purpose in our lives. Why we have had to experience violence is not clear, but in many cases, our purpose can grow from that experience and lift us up beyond our current circumstances. Sometimes I find having purpose in my life means just getting up in the morning to being the best I can be so I can inspire others.

TAWANDA

Five years from now, I don't think I'll be at the same job. I'll still be working in the human services field, though, and looking for a location for my shopping mall space. I'll still have so many steps to accomplish yet to get to my bigger goal, a vision I had in Susan's workshop about a developing a strip mall with a daycare center, a hair salon, a diner and a playscape. It all came to me so vividly because of my experience as a single mom with three children. With all the credentials I have now and ones that will be coming, I can see how doors can open up for me to many other options and possibilities.

TENNILLE

Now that I am thriving and living well, my life goals are so different than from when I was just surviving. I didn't think about how I wanted to help people with my nursing skills until I saw myself as a thriver. I can see today how working in the nursing field has brought different things up from my childhood. It has made me realize I was meant to be do something to help kids.

Working in school nursing and then pediatrics as I have, I can see the warning signs with the kids and how certain behaviors show me that something has happened to them. I am able to help families parent their children, and that is so purposeful to me. Maybe that's because no one did that for me when I was a kid. I'm not blaming anyone, but I tell my kids "I love you. God bless you and don't let anyone touch your body!" That little snippet is so important. No one ever told me not to let anyone touch my body, so how would I have known that? We know that kind of trauma in childhood can affect all of our future relationships.

Having my associate's degree in nursing and being in Susan's Thriver Community have helped me to move toward my long-term goal of working with women and children to help them to take their own journey beyond abuse. With my eye on having my BSN (bachelor's degree in nursing) in five years, followed by an APRN (Advanced Practice Registered Nurse), I know I can do it. My goals are attainable now.

What follows next in Part Four of this book are the full interviews from each of the women, but first below is the full list of questions I asked them in those interviews. At the end of Part Five, check out the quick quiz you can take – *Are You Living in the Thriver Zone?* – by which you can measure and celebrate your own progress for living in your happily-ever-after!

I hope that you are inspired by the stories of these seven women and the many women mentioned throughout this book and other books in *The Thriver Zone Series*™. They have been eager to move beyond abuse and I am pleased that the materials I have developed has helped them set a new vision for their lives and then step into that vision. Without a dream, you can't make a dream come true!

We are thrivers!

Part Four

THE LIST OF QUESTIONS ASKED
FOR THE THRIVER SUCCESS STORIES IN PART FOUR

Thanks to Adrienne, Cathryn, Jenny, Pamela, Sophia, Tawanda, Tennille!

1. When you first came to work with Susan in her *My Avenging Angel Workshops*™, how were you feeling about yourself and your future? Did you believe your future was going to be bright and good? Or did you not believe that your life would ever get better?

2. What obstacles did you have in your life at that time to having a bright future? Did you think you could overcome those obstacles?

3. In her workshops, Susan talks about all of us being on a journey from victim to survivor to thriver. Does that journey make sense to you? How were you convinced? What difference did that knowledge of the journey make in your life?

4. What exercises from the workshop helped you the most?
    - The Seven Steps to Thriving After Abuse (See your Journey, Quiet Inner Critic, Connect with Happy Person Inside You, Get Positive Energy, Vision a New Life, Overcome Fears, Set New Goals)
    - A Road Map to Manifest a Life of Power and Purpose.

5. What does being a thriver mean to you? Who are your thriver role models?

6. How has it helped you on your journey to thriving to be a part of Susan's Thriver Community? What activities in the Thriver Community have helped you the most to keep thriving?

7. What things do you do in your life to keep yourself in the Thriver Zone?

8. What tips do you have for women on taking the journey from victim to survivor to thriver?

9. What do you wish you would have known earlier in your life about the journey from victim to survivor to thriver? Describe your life today as a thriver. How does it feel?

10. What does the idea that "Living Well Is the Best Revenge" mean to you?

11. Have you been able to live well as a thriver? What's one thing you thought you couldn't accomplish but you did? What do you still want to do? What are your goals?

12. Have you been able to find a life of power and purpose as a thriver? Describe it. How are you a Woman of Power? How have you found a purpose for your life, a reason why you are here on this earth right now?

~ ~ ~ ~ ~ ~ ~ ~ ~ ~ ~ ~ ~ ~ ~

*Be the hero of your own story.
Show the world the quality of your character,
the strength of your resolve and the size of your heart.*

— GARY RYAN BLAIR

Part Four

THRIVER SUCCESS STORIES

Adrienne

*The biggest adventure you can ever take is
to live the life of your dreams.*

— Oprah Winfrey

FROM THE BEGINNING

When I first came to one of Susan's workshop in November of 2012, I thought that I was doing pretty good. I had been divorced since 2005, and I was working in a full-time job as well as teaching part-time. While I was still recovering financially from my divorce, I thought I was in a better place overall. But Susan helped me see that I was really very good at surviving but not much more than that. In fact, I was a "high-functioning" survivor. It might have felt like I was moving forward, but actually I was vacillating between victim to survivor. I didn't even know what "thriving" was.

True, I had come a long way from the years of being a victim, and I survived a marriage with an abusive partner. When we divorced, there was a long, drawn-out custody battle over our children, and financially there were days when my children were young that I struggled to find ways to feed them and myself. We were so poor! When I met Susan, I was doing the best I could, but it was always a struggle. I was nowhere close to thriving.

SEVEN STEPS TO THRIVING

What I learned from Susan was that to get to thriving, I had to get positive energy into my life. Every step of Susan's *Seven Steps to Thriving After Abuse* helped me to do that. *The First Step: See the Journey* helped me see where I wanted to go and that I wanted to be a thriver.

The *Second Step: Quiet the Inner Critic* became so important to me because I didn't know that the voice inside me that constantly criticized me and put me down was my Inner Critic. I also learned that the Inner Critic was only one of the voices in my head and that I could drown the Inner Critic by using the *Third Step: Connect with the Happy Person Inside You.* That is the part of me untouched by anything that had ever happened to me, and it brought me to *Step Four: Get Positive Energy* and *Step Five: Vision a New Life.* With those positive thoughts and emotions, I could vision a new future for myself with unlimited possibilities. What a thought! Learning how to use all these steps together was a healing moment for me.

Then with *Step Six: Overcome Fears*, I was able to see that the limiting beliefs about myself were connected to the Inner Critic, and when they came up as fears, I could combat them with positive affirmations. That way even little fears wouldn't turn into big ones and, in fact, Susan helped me see that I already had a positive pattern of overcoming fear in the past. I could use that pattern to confront my present-day fears and work toward the vision I have for a better, more positive future. Finally, in *Step Seven: Set New Goals,* Susan's suggestion that we start from the last thing we'd need to do to accomplish our goal down to the first gave me the confidence that I could achieve my goals step-by-step.

MY ACCOMPLISHMENTS AS A THRIVER

Since meeting Susan, I have become pretty adept at manifesting my goals. Manifesting was also a new word that Susan taught me. She showed me that with positive energy, a focused desire and by overcoming my fears, I could manifest my dreams. In doing so, I was able to move my life forward and thrive! Working all of the Seven Steps to Thriving After Abuse together also gave me a better sense of how amazing my Inner Being was and how she wanted me to have a life of power and purpose in this lifetime.

Sure, I had the potential to do this work before I met Susan, but my head was jumbled up with so many conflicting messages about myself and my worth. These thoughts are a result of the abuse and trauma I have experienced in my life. Susan's *Seven Steps to Thriving After Abuse* gave me a way work around the effects of PTSD, depression and anxiety in my life so I could manifest my desires and live the life of a thriver. I also learned that I didn't always have to follow the order of the steps, particularly when I needed to quiet the Inner Critic and bring up the positive energy of the Happy Person Inside. Those are two steps I always come back to.

With the tools that Susan gave me, I found myself doing big things, things that have allowed me to transform myself every few years. I can recognize now that when the Inner Critic gets loud, I'll say to myself, "Oh! That's my Inner Critic" and deal with it, getting myself back on track. What I found is that when I'm not being held down by my own fears, I can open up to the possibility that anything is possible and live my life to the fullest. That's how I try to live my life now every day!

Starting a Business

The first goal I accomplished as a thriver was to manifest a business working with essential oils. After being introduced to the oils in a class, I soon became more and more passionate about working with them. I loved the medicinal use of them, but I also had fun with the aromatic side. Actually, essential oils heal on many levels – spiritual, emotional, mental and physical – all at once. So I might be drawn to sniff lavender today when I have a sore throat, but it's also good for just about everything. But it also calms my nerves, and I need that right now. So essential oils can work on all those levels, and you can't miss because when you are helping all those levels feel better, your energy is naturally going to rise like a balloon into the sky. When I started making gifts with the oils for people and they loved how they worked for them, I was asked for more, so slowly I turned my passion into a business. Looking back I can see that my introduction to essential oils and the business I have grown from my passionate interest in them would have never happened without Susan guiding me.

Getting My Master's Degree

Another of my passions was inspired by a woman in Susan's Thriver Community. I was making bead bracelets at the time, and she wanted one. When I delivered it to her, we talked for a while, and she told me she had gotten her master's degree. That impressed me, and as I drove home in my car that day, something inside me said out loud, "Wow, Adrienne! You could get your master's degree too." Don't you know it, in four years' time, I had a master's degree. The challenging part was deciding what I wanted to study, and that took me a couple years to figure out. I knew I didn't want a business degree, but when I heard about a school for integrated health and healing,

I knew it was perfect for me. I had been working in the medical field for a while, and I was excited to integrate that medical knowledge with the holistic healing methods I had been learning, including energy healing. So I became a Reiki master and also an Integrated Energy Healing master instructor.

Finding Laughter Yoga, Energy Work

Laughter yoga was the first energy modality that I got certified in. When I first did laughter yoga, I learned that breathing from the diaphragm allows your body to be saturated with oxygen. After breathing like that at my first laughter yoga session, I realized I was so oxygen deprived. I was literally on cloud nine with oxygen flowing through my body, and it stayed there for almost two days! It was so profoundly different than the gray life I had been living! All of a sudden, I was into vibrant colors and jumping up and down. I felt ten years younger. I thought, *I have to do this laughter yoga again.* So I did, and I knew I had to get certified as an instructor. I loved it so much. It was really big step for me, and it got me going.

Then I was drawn into other energy work. I was called to channel the angelic realm, and that set me on a course of study. I love studying! I also explored energy healing touch; nurses have developed and use this in their practice, so I found nothing unusual about using it too. We all have energy coursing through us, and sometimes our energy is blocked by all the things that have happened to us. That energy needs to get unblocked, and when it is, that's when the healing begins.

THE THRIVER COMMUNITY

All of my accomplishments as a thriver helped me to get positive energy, and the higher my energy level was, the more fun I was having. Soon everything fell into place perfectly. I learned that you have to vibrate at the level of what you want to achieve because positive attracts positive. You have to allow the positive to come. Susan's follow-up group for the women who complete her two-day workshop was very important in helping me to keep my positive energy flowing.

Since all the women in this Thriver Community, like me, have experienced some kind of abuse and now we are moving beyond it, we have a strong, common bond – stronger than family for me. When you are with others in Susan's Thriver Community, you get energy just from being in the same room. I have become a role model and mentor in the group, even though I don't want people to think I'm better than anyone else. I was thriving so much, accomplishing so many of my goals, that I needed to share my progress with other like-minded women in the group. The women wanted to know how I did it, and I needed their support and friendship.

Now I work every day to keep my energy up by smiling to myself and learning to like myself. I didn't like myself very much for most of my life, so I was always very depressed, and I struggled to feel anything positive. Everyone knows what low energy is like – you are lethargic, sad and anxious. You feel like you can't stand up or walk, like you are being held down. But to raise my energy, I smile, laugh, sing in the car and clap my hands – anything to feel positive – and suddenly my energy soars. It might start with a smile on my face at the oddest moment, and some people might think I'm a little crazy, but not in my reality, positive always wins the day!

LIVING WELL

Today, I am living well, and that has been my best revenge! My living well is that I wake up in the morning, feeling happy and grateful for everything that I have. Being positive now is just my way of being. Living well for me is also realizing that I am safe and secure, whole and complete just as I am. It took a long time for this kind of positive thinking to seep into my soul. The more I show gratitude and grace, the more I receive. Now that I am able to bring up positive energy into my life every day, I feel so different. I realize that if what you do, think and say makes you feel good, you can create positive energy in your own soul.

Right now, I'm working on changing where I live. I found a place on the ocean where I can spend time and process things in my life after the recent deaths of my father and brother. I want to revive my healing business and make products again with essential oils. I want to do workshops and talk to groups about the ways you can raise your energy, keep yourself calm, bring down your anxiety and ease your depression. You could call this work a kind of life coaching, but I also love my essential oils. They are important part of this work, and they are calling me to heal the world.

A LIFE OF POWER AND PURPOSE

By living well, I have found a life of power and purpose as a thriver. The longer I live in the Thriver Zone, the more I am able to feel my power. Having been abused or suffering trauma in your life can make you a bit meek. You want to be empowered to take your live forward and see a new vision for yourself. This is not the kind of power over you or that can be used against you to control you and make you feel bad. Instead, you are empowered to change your life and the lives of others so that everyone has the opportunity to live well.

My purpose in life changes all the time. Right now, my purpose is to make myself happy. I've spent many, many years taking care of others, so now I want a calm place to live and to heal myself for my next act in life. I know that what's next is going to be big because I'm always going to dream big – bigger and bigger – now that I am thriving! This is truly my best revenge – making bigger and bigger dreams come true each day!

– Adrienne

How I Know I Am a Thriver

by Adrienne

I know I am a thriver because I can look at myself the mirror and see a happy face! My eyes are blue again, and there is happiness there now where before there was only gray and sadness. Yes, that's right – my eyes have changed back to their God-given color: blue.

My journey has been long, a dozen years. How did I get here? Someone literally took me by the hand to guide me in my first step. At first, I was only a living, breathing body just getting through each day. Those who know can relate. We spend our days just getting by, trying not to make our abusers angry, which is impossible, but we try with all our hearts anyway. We raise our children, keep house, make meals and work, but there is no joy and no emotion other than fear.

I know I am a thriver because I now feel joy when I wake up in the morning!

Joy! Joy! Joy! Joy to be alive, joy to work, joy to see my children grow to be adults.

I know I am a thriver because I see color in the world again! The world is a rainbow!

I know I am a thriver because I love my body! It is mine, not someone else's to ravage and throw away when they are done with it. I had accumulated sixty pounds of protection which I no longer need and has slipped away. I feel beautiful!

I know I am a thriver because I am able to help others see their beauty! In the abusive situation, I could not even help myself, but now I can help others on their journey, and this brings even more joy!

I know I am a thriver because I can laugh again. Not just any kind of laughter – rich belly laughter that oxygenates my brain and my soul, bringing more joy!

I know I am a thriver because I have a deep connection to God! I am connected to all living beings on earth; the angels told me. I see concrete signs of this connection every day!

I know I am a thriver because I am not afraid to dream again! I am the snake. I have shed the skin of fear of my dreams, and they come to me now and provide me messages of joy!

I know I am a thriver because I am grateful for everything in my life, all of it, the good and not so good. The challenges have helped me be more grateful for the abundance I have now.

I know I am a thriver because I have learned to forgive. Forgiveness of self is the highest mountain to climb; I am almost at the summit. Even forgiveness of the abuser is necessary to thrive. This is the teaching of God, and it is so.

~ ~ ~ ~ ~ ~ ~ ~ ~ ~ ~ ~ ~ ~ ~ ~

A goal is a dream with a deadline.
— NAPOLEON HILL

THRIVER SUCCESS STORIES

Cathryn

When we bring what is within out into the world, miracles happen.

— Henry David Thoreau

FROM THE BEGINNING

When I first came to one of Susan's workshops in March 2016, I didn't feel good about myself. So many people's words had beaten me down for so long. I like to think about where I was on a "human wellness" scale. That would be a line from left to right, ranging from death on the left to thriving with vitality on the right. A person very near death would be almost submerged underground on the left, their head barely poking out. Farther to the right would be a person slowly climbing out of that hole in the ground. All the way to the right side, a person would be bursting with energy, jumping up and down with a zest and joy for life.

Where was I on that on that wellness scale when I met Susan? I certainly wasn't thriving on the right side of the scale. I wasn't full of joy for life. I'd say that when I came to Susan's workshop, I had emerged a little bit from being underground on the far left of the line, but that ground was like quicksand that keeps sucking you down. With quicksand, you have to work really, really hard to get out, and it doesn't help when you feel like you have a ton of people who are pushing you down further into that quicksand rather than helping you get out.

That's the way I saw my life. The initial abuse – domestic violence in my relationship with my husband at the time – had pushed me down. But when I spoke up to people and told them what I was going through in my marriage, they would either disbelieve me or blame me for what had happened. It was their actions that revictimized me and pushed me down further.

Part Four

When I came to Susan's workshop, I felt like one or both of my legs were still stuck in that quicksand! My head wasn't totally underground, but some days it felt like it was. I came looking for supportive, nonjudgmental people, feeling very alone on my journey. I felt like the whole cultural community in the church I was raised in had turned against me because of the accusations of abuse I brought up against my husband, who was also part of the same church. Speaking up about abuse was simply not okay. The message I kept getting from other people was: "You're not perfect either," and "You need to forgive and forget," and "You're not right!" That stumped me. *What do you mean, I'm not right? I'm not right about my own experience?*

Still I wondered, *Maybe I'm not right. Maybe I'm exaggerating this. Am I really?* When I would go back and revisit the things that had happened, I'd wonder what was really true. My reality shifted. I didn't even know what was what anymore.

Susan has a writing exercise she uses called "The Hero's Journey." (See more about this exercise in Part Two of this book.) It's about setting forth on an important task, encountering monumental obstacles, and then pushing through to ultimately succeed. In response to this writing prompt, I wrote a poem entitled "This Is Wrong" to tell the story of my first realization that what I was going through was abuse, and then how, after speaking up about it, I was re-victimized by other people's reactions to my speaking out. The poem shows how their words knocked me down further, yet I pushed through that devastation to become strong again, just like the hero reaps a reward at the end of the Hero's Journey.

But once you are down, the revictimization is even worse than the initial abuse. When something bad happens to you, normally you can get support and understanding from others, and that can soothe the pain. But when the people you go to for help hurt you by disbelieving you or blaming you for what happened, that hurt can knock you further into the ground than the initial abuse. It's like a child sexual abuse survivor telling a parent what happened to them and the parent disbelieving them or blaming them. That is so much worse than when a child is believed and the perpetrator is held accountable.

This poem is the journey of my voice being beaten down and then coming back in a powerful way.

THIS IS WRONG

by Cathryn

It's just a whisper, just a thought, just a blip across my conscious mind...
this is wrong

I question myself as others do too.
I believe the lie that they must know me better than I know myself.

I say it aloud in private, alone
I try out the words, feel them as they slip through my lips.
this is wrong

I let the thought linger longer in my mind.
It collides against self-realization and new understanding
sticks to the words as they become bigger, more powerful.
this is wrong

I finally believe it enough to speak up and tell someone else.
My voice is hesitant, needing validation.
This is wrong, I try to assert.

The words come back: "You think you're right! But you are wrong! You've no right to fight!"
They push me down and criticize, think they're seeing through my eyes.
The words beat me down and I retreat inside my shell – admit defeat.
They tumble around and knock my self-concept off balance.
I yield, I break, I lose part of myself.
Am I wrong?

The anchor tied around me tight,
Keeps me held down deep. Don't talk, don't fight.
I've lost myself and in despair, I cry to God, I know he cares.
He brings angel hands that help me bear
This pain, this throbbing heartache of having *no voice.*

Part Four

I find supporters, believers, validators.
Their words are healing…and soon I start to see truth again.
Broken and devastated, the safest place I knew is gone.
Cracked and chipped, but pieced together, I rise again and find my voice.
This is wrong

Again the insults slam my face. They try to enter sacred space
But I don't believe these critics now. Instead…I'm led
Back to the truth. I stand up tall.
God told me I am valuable and worthy of love and respect.
I shut out everything else and believe him.
And I start to hear the words inside
Rise up like a volcano's blast.
This is wrong

I disbelieve the others' lies.
They don't know – to truth they're blind.
Now my insides start to scream. I know my truth! I know what's me!
And this is wrong!

They want to silence every ounce of strength I've gained.
They want to pounce and hold me down. Remove my roar and break me – yet again.
But I am strong, no longer afraid of powers that be
Or the punishments they can give to me.
I say it over and over again
This is wrong!

I am bruised but I am brave.
I am who I'm meant to be. This is me!
I shout out loud, my calling clear.
I own my voice in spite of fear.
The way ahead is hard but bright.
I will shout loudly! I will fight!
This is wrong!

Finding my voice and coming back in this powerful way, I am now at the point that I am strong enough to help other people. I had to first fully believe my own reality so that I could help others in similar situations. I understand where other women are coming from when they speak out about abuse, and I hear people say victim-blaming statements all the time. They say, "It takes two," or "She just needs to get over it." Or she should have done this or that differently to not provoke him.

I can identify with all those accusations, and I remember what it's like to be in a spot where pain and trauma can affect you so adversely. For example, a friend of mine who was so beaten down by the abuse in her life developed rheumatoid arthritis. Sometimes she can hardly function, and at times when I stop over to her house, it can be very messy. I could see how some people might say, "Why doesn't she get her act together and clean up her house?" I remember people saying such things to me.

To me that is so wrong. You need to meet a victim where she is and just help. Sometimes I'll go see her and do the dishes if my friend is okay with that. Over the past few years, I've noticed that she has gotten stronger, and every time I go there, her house is a little bit cleaner, not because I told her clean her house, but because she's stronger. So for victims to get out of that victim place, we need support, not condemnation. I want to be part of that support because I know how it feels to have no support. I also know how finally finding the right kind of support enabled me to get my strength back.

JOURNEY TO THRIVING

My journey beyond abuse has been about moving from surviving to thriving in my life. What thriving means to me is taking care of myself so well that I have energy to help others.

When I was just surviving, it took all my strength to keep my head above water and just live life day-to-day. I was taking from others and not giving anything back. I wouldn't have known what to do if I found another person who was struggling. I had no energy to help them, and I even wondered if I would ever get to a place where I would. But I found supportive people to help me, and after being on the receiving end of their help, I was able to make the journey beyond abuse to now be filled with life and energy. I have more than enough for my own life now, and I can give back to others who need it since I understand what they are going through.

When I was in that energy-depleted victim place, I had no idea how I would get my energy back. Was that even possible? I didn't see a life beyond feeling powerless and hopeless, or a future filled with adventures or positive, joyful things. I once believed that I could have that kind of life, but it had got beaten out of me over the course of the abuse. I only saw enough to put one foot in front of the other, plod through and deal with all the challenges. Actually, the revictimization was by far the greatest challenge in what it did to my self-concept, making me doubt myself and reality.

SETTING A VISION

Back when I was feeling powerless from the abuse I had experienced, I did not see a future for myself of fulfilling adventures. But once I realized in Susan's workshops that I was on a journey that could take me beyond just surviving, I felt I could take my power back, get strong enough to live a great life and even help others. The exercise Susan had us do in *Step Five: Vision a New Life* helped me set a vision to do exactly that.

I loved imagining myself in the future with my Happy Person Inside, who we were introduced to in *Step Three: Connect with the Happy Person Inside You.* We wrote about being in that future as if it was the present time. One of the dreams I wrote about in this visioning exercise was about me conducting a retreat on a quiet, peaceful lake with mountains all around for women who have been through abuse. I love being around mountains and lakes, and I still envision different variations on that dream, including having a nonprofit organization to financially support women on "healing journeys" and adventurous trips.

So many women I have encountered who experienced abuse don't have money to go on a vacation. With payments I have received regularly from my husband post-separation, I can do that. I can take a week away and do something to replenish myself when my kids are with their dad. I am so thankful I have that. So many women don't. I would love to see them be able to travel and take trips, maybe combining it with a therapeutic element. I'm studying psychology now, and so many of the things I have learned about the human experience I would love to teach and impart to other women.

I'm also a Life Skills facilitator, and I teach a combination of all different kind of therapies in an educational model, not a therapeutic one. I teach women coping skills and how to deal with things that trigger you emotionally. I'm also being trained in the Nonviolent Communication technique developed by Marshall Rosenberg which is a kind of nonjudgmental communication using tag lines like "When I heard you say… this is how it felt," that works so much better than confrontation. You can communicate in a way that the other person doesn't feel attacked or on edge.

MOST HELPFUL EXERCISES

Learning to set a vision for the future in my healing process has opened me up to things that I never thought I would do or be interested in. Because of that, I started a dream journal, writing down for a whole year all the dreams I have for what I want to do in my life. I had to get past the point of thinking that if I wrote something down, I had to do it. I allowed myself the freedom to write whatever I thought of, and if I ever do it or not, it's okay. That freed me to see that there can be a future with all kinds of possibilities. I don't know what I'm going to end up doing, but it's okay to dream and tell myself that I can do anything if I put the effort in. At times I do procrastinate or I don't want to do something, but I've stopped telling myself, "Okay, that's a nice thought, but you are never going to do that." Now I realize I can do whatever I decide to by finding the resources and people to help me.

Another exercise in Susan's *Seven Steps to Thriving After Abuse* that I found very helpful was *Step Two: Quiet the Inner Critic.* So many negative voices had gotten inside my head telling me I was worthless that I have to be active in countering these negative thoughts. I started to use the exercise Susan does with us on this step in her workshops in my daily life. When a negative thought comes up, I write it down on a piece of paper. Then I draw a line down the center of the page, and on the other side of that line, I write the truth. For example, my husband told me he was mad that I was taking the kids to Florida after we were separated. He said the kids would miss their friends at home, and they were going to have an awful time in Florida. With all that negativity swirling around in my head, I couldn't help but think, *Is he right? Is that the truth? Are they going to miss their friends so much that they are going wish that they didn't go with me?* On the other side of the line, I wrote the truth in the most positive way I could. "We are going to Florida, and we're going to have an awesome time. It doesn't matter what he thinks!" Countering it with my truth allowed me to let it go of the negativity and visualize the positive.

I have progressed tremendously in this process of quieting my Inner Critic. At first, to stop the negative thoughts in my head, I had to write down both the negative and positive. Now I don't write anything down. I recognize a thought as negative, counter it with the truth in my head, and move on. Shortcutting that process shows where I am today as a thriver. My truth is much more solid, like a wall, and negative thoughts rarely even enter my space. When people say negative things to me, I think, *Okay, that's about them. They are having a bad day. That's not about me.* Sometimes a negative thought can even be disguised in a genuinely caring way such as "I care about you. That's why I'm trying to help you manage your life better." In other words, they are saying that I need to be fixed. But I tell myself, "Forget about it; they don't even know my life." I'm very lucky that I don't have that kind of negativity in my head naturally. Most of the negative thoughts have come from other people. But when it does come from within, I have learned to recognize quickly how certain things in my past have hurt me and made me think that I wasn't valuable. Now I'm moving past that, learning that I have value and worth and that I deserve to be treated with respect. That was a huge milestone for me.

WHAT MAKES ME HAPPY

Another exercise in *Step Four: Get Positive Energy* has also been helpful to me. I needed to learn the ways I get positive energy so I could build up my strength, overcome obstacles and challenges and not feel so powerless. I needed my power back – not power over anyone else, but my own power to enable me to live my own life well. In this step, Susan has us write about what makes us happy and how we feel before, during and after we do it. If we haven't done it in a long time, then she suggests that we go do it and then write about it afterward.

I love hiking. I love being on the top of a mountain looking out and down on everything. That is the best! It really fills me up. I also like being out in nature in general as well as singing and listening to music that fills me with joy and energy. Realizing now what makes me happy means that I can now more easily take that journey from feeling down and discouraged to being mostly filled with joy all the time. That's where I am now. I go do something I love to do, such as hike a mountain or listen to music for two hours, and then I feel so much better. I find that if I'm down, I really need two hours hiking or being in nature. One hour doesn't seem to do it for me. Two hours listening to songs works for me. The first hour I may be barely singing the words, but by the end of the second hour, I'm totally filled with joy again.

A big part of my ability to find joy like this is in my faith in God. He fills me with strength, joy, love and all the positive things I value. But I always need that two hours. A brief prayer won't do it, but if I am really down and struggling, two hours gets me out. Learning that about myself was huge because now I know that I don't have to be stuck in that down place anymore. If I am feeling low, I take two hours of my time, even if it means listening to music while I'm just doing the dishes!

Two hours is a lot of time in our world, but we need to care about ourselves enough to do it. To me, that is all part of thriving – taking time for myself. Europeans take all kinds of vacations. They take the whole month of August off! We Americans work all the time, but we need to replenish ourselves so we can stay and live in the Thriver Zone. Taking time for myself to be filled with joy and hope is what gives me strength and power.

THE THRIVER COMMUNITY

What has helped me the most on my healing journey has been the support I found, including Susan's follow-up group for women who complete her two-day workshop. I have done other programs that were ten-week sessions start to finish, and then you never see anyone again. I liked having a permanent community in Susan's program whenever you need it.

I don't always attend the monthly events or the annual weekend retreats of Susan's Thriver Community but knowing that they are there and getting the emails from Susan about them gives me feel a sense of being grounded. If I need this place, it is there, an enveloping cocoon of nonjudgmental support when things get difficult in my life. I love to go to the events whenever I can because it's so helpful for me to feel this sense of community and belonging. These women might have a lifestyle or culture totally different than mine, but there is a commonality of overcoming abuse. I feel a sense of acceptance that I don't necessarily have anywhere else. There are other people who are really close to me in my life, but they don't understand that part of my experience. If they walked with me while I was on that part of my journey, they may understand what I've gone through pretty well, but it's still not the same as someone who has actually been through it.

Another thing I like about Susan's Thriver Community is that we don't spend time talking about our stories. Susan makes sure that we are safe, and if we are in need of crisis intervention services at any time, she'll make a referral to a domestic violence or sexual assault intervention program or other resources that can help women on the first part of the journey from victim to survivor.

When I first came out of the abuse as a survivor, I definitely needed to go to those types of programs and talk about what actually happened to me. I also journaled a lot about my experiences. I had to write or talk about my story as many times as I needed in order to resolve it in my own head, but I didn't want to stay there forever. In Susan's Thriver Community, you take the journey from survivor to thriver. We know that you've been through a difficult past and that you don't want to get stuck in that negative energy forever. In the Thriver Community, you are accepted for who you are and your past is a given, but it doesn't define you anymore.

MY THRIVER ACCOMPLISHMENTS

Getting to a place of physical safety was huge for me at the start of my journey. But once I felt that safety and started moving beyond the abuse, I needed to find people and places where I would be emotionally safe too. Susan's workshops and follow-up activities are that emotionally safe place for me. It is a supportive social group where I don't have to constantly explain myself and everyone there understands that sometimes we can be triggered back into a bad space, but we don't have to stay there. For me, once I had an emotionally safe space, I could start imagining a life free from fear and free from being controlled. I could take control of my own life and make my own choices. For me, that was my journey out of abuse, through being a survivor and on to becoming a thriver and living well!

When I moved into the thriver part of my journey, I gave myself permission to dream freely and imagine all my possibilities. This opened up new worlds for me and made realize that I am finally no longer just surviving and using all my energy to get through the day. I'm on another part of the journey, no longer seeking help from others but now able to help others who are in a place of fear and powerlessness.

To do that, I have been working with Lundy Bancroft, author of several books, most notably *Why Does He Do That? Inside the Minds of Angry, Controlling Men.* Being connected with him has given me an opportunity to talk with experts and lawyers around the country about how to work with and help women who are victims of domestic violence.

For example, since lawyers do not typically understand the dynamics of abuse, I will educate them on the ways that legal abuse occurs in court settings. I explain how to help victims they represent by understanding their reactions to the trauma they have experienced and how to keep them safe by not giving in to things that will continue to victimize them. One common legal abuse scenario is a mother bringing up abuse of the children in court, but then having the abuser accuse her of making it up. Frequently guardians ad litem will believe him instead of her, and if her lawyer is not educated on abuse, he may ask the victim, "Are you really sure?" That question coming from her own attorney is the last thing she needs.

FINDING MY ROLE

My role, given my experience as a victim of domestic violence, is to try to help the lawyers and experts understand dynamics like this so that they can represent their clients fully. I would never have pictured myself in such a role or being connected to someone famous like Lundy. But this work has allowed me to help women across the country, and it has been very empowering for me. I am helping in a way I never would have envisioned back at the beginning of my journey.

What I still want to accomplish is for the many women in my native culture and church community who are being abused to have a safe place to speak up and get help. I feel that the Christian values of submission and peace are at times used against women to keep them in fear and oppression. Submission alone doesn't have to be a negative thing, but submission and force should never be used together against women. You may choose to submit because you value something or you are asked in a kind way to do something. But submission should never be a part of oppression, and the appearance of peace at all costs should not be pushed in a Christian community. I see the need to do more education in Christian communities on what abuse is. Some of that is being done but not much in my own denomination.

Recently I started a support group for women in our churches. We had our first retreat last summer, and some of the women with whom I connected had not realized they were in abusive relationships. There are other women in similar situations who still aren't free to talk about it within their church communities. I want to change that by educating the Christian community, especially ours, that abuse in a relationship does not align with the values in the Bible and how these situations could be handled appropriately when they come up. In some cases they are handled very well, with the women finding support and help in their church without being blamed for what happened. In other cases, like mine, it has been exactly the opposite.

WHAT CAN CHANGE

There needs to be more consistency in our denomination about how these situations are dealt with, and the knowledge gained about domestic violence needs to be more than just learning, for example, that name calling and yelling without physical violence is also abuse. The leaders, especially the ones who may be approached in these situations, should be trained in safety planning so that they learn about the dynamics of power and control in a relationship and how women might react. For example, a woman might lash out in response to the abuse, but focusing on her behavior alone won't help. Nor will ignoring the fact that the abuser's behavior can be seen in a number of ways depending on one's relationship to him.

Recently, I got a comment from an elder in my church who said, "I had a conversation with your husband, and he's so reasonable." First, I would like him to understand that he might be reasonable with you, but pushing me to get back together with him because he is so reasonable to you is not helpful. Second, everyone can be reasonable some of the time, and some of the time they are not. Third, you may see that side of him, but then if I come to you and say that these other bad things are happening too, I need help.

The church leaders also need to understand that joint counseling is detrimental in these situations. We were pushed into that by the church. They also need to believe victims even when the abuser denies the allegations. Don't just believe an abuser because he is a man. Listen to the allegations. Assume they are true if you don't know otherwise and help the victim in whatever way you can.

Church leaders also need to learn that they must continually confront and hold abusers accountable. Like a recovering alcoholic, the abuser will probably always have that tendency, but if they have accountability in a loving way, they may be able to change their behavior. Accountability done in a punitive way won't work, because this is a person, too, and we need to have compassion on them.

WHAT IS A THRIVER?

Thriving to me means taking care of myself so well that I have energy to help others, even those who have hurt me. To me this is the ultimate level of thriving. Forgiving those who hurt you, I believe, is very important because it may release you from overwhelming feelings, but you don't have to forgive and forget. While you may not want vengeance or for evil things to happen to them, you do have to be safe, take care of and protect yourself, and this includes remembering. You can't go blindly sticking your finger in the light socket over and over again.

Forgiving someone for their actions toward you can be a way of you releasing your anger about their actions toward you. That is a process I have been working through around the anger I have felt toward a church elder who, in his handling of my situation, revictimized me more than the abuse by my husband. I have to get to the point of finally releasing that anger, although I feel like I have already released my bitterness. The anger is still there now for a purpose because I'm working on getting changes made, and my anger is propelling me to complete that. But it is not obscuring my compassion for him. I can feel anger and love at the same time. Bitterness is a lot stronger. I couldn't even listen to his sermons when I was bitter. Caring about him is how I got out of the bitterness.

Feeling compassion even to those who have hurt me is the ultimate level of thriving to me. It is a level of integrity that comes from being whole. Thriving is living within my own personal power while still respecting all others. Even if I am angry at those who hurt me, I still choose to treat them with respect and compassion. That is a very important value to me.

Part of my goal with the church community is to educate others about the dynamics of domestic violence in a variety of different ways. Right now, I have been working on writing a book about my experience, and I have a website in mind that can educate both victims and church leaders alike. I'd also like to initiate policy reform within my church and other denominations to address the needs of victims of domestic violence and help leaders be more aware of the impact of domestic violence on victims as well as the children.

LIVING WELL

While I like the quote "Living well is the best revenge," I like to focus on living well, not on revenge. My goal is to model for others what living well is, even for those in my life who have hurt me. I don't want them to stay stuck there, and I don't want to be angry at them. I want them to see that living well means taking control of your life. You are not in control of yourself when you are trying to control others.

I have this vision: There is an ocean, and I am a dolphin out in the ocean, just totally free. At the beginning of my journey, I was not free. I was in a net. Now I am out in the ocean, swimming around freely. I can go anywhere I want and do whatever I want because I am free. There is nobody forcing me out of fear, or control or whatever to do what they say I have to do. I can choose to do whatever I want to.

Somewhere is my husband with whom I still have this connection; we have kids together. I have this commitment and a connection to him still, but I'm not allowing myself to be under his control anymore. I'm willing to submit, but only if what he asks is good and right. In my vision, he's in a little boat somewhere trying to catch me. I'm out in this ocean, a dolphin, totally free. What's so huge for me is that his little boat can't catch a dolphin!

Being the dolphin in this situation makes me feel like no one can hold power over me anymore because I know who I am, God loves me and I have a purpose. The only way that he and I will ever be together again will not be if he gets me in the boat because I'm not going there, but only if he gets out of the boat and becomes a dolphin too. So if he is ever finally free of the constraints in his own life – the obstacles, the fears, the control, all of his past that he hasn't dealt with – he can get to that free spot too. Then we can both be dolphins swimming in the ocean.

Hope is a huge value to me, and it empowers me. It's part of my Christian values, but anyone can have hope. Whenever I think in my mind that something is not possible, I don't even entertain that thought. I go right to the thought that all things are possible. I really firmly believe that when you have that kind of belief in infinite possibilities, more things happen. With those who have abused me, I choose to model that kind of hope and faith for them. I have to be smarter at detecting the abusive tactics and work on changes in the system that are more compassionate for victims and perpetrators alike. I can see that abusers gain power when their behavior is reinforced by the system, while the victim's power is diminished when their experiences are distorted, ignored or dismissed.

A LIFE OF POWER AND PURPOSE

Susan's program has helped me to see that after experiencing abuse and being revictimized by the systems around me, I still had value. I could have a good future and take my power back. Today, I am a woman of power. As a Christian, I get my power from Jesus Christ. Negative words from people cannot come between me and the love and value that I have from Him. That is definitely the Real Me.

Finding the Real Me has given me a purpose in life. I want to help victims of domestic violence take the journey beyond abuse so they can thrive as I have. One of the ways I have begun to fulfill this purpose is to work on completing my bachelor's degree in psychology. My studies in this field have helped me to shape the dreams and ideas I have for how to do this work.

One of my dreams is to get a master's degree in policy writing or nonprofit administration. I'm leaning toward policy because I did a policy-writing class last spring and loved it. I've always loved to do puzzles, and to me, policy writing is like solving a puzzle. You take all these bits and pieces and come up with something that really works. As I go through life as a survivor, I see different systems, whether it's the police, insurance or courts, and I'll come across something and think, *Wait! That doesn't work for domestic violence survivors the way you have it set up.*

For example, I had to submit claims to our health insurance company for taking my daughter to the hospital emergency room. My husband is the primary on our insurance, so they sent the reimbursement payment on the claim to him even though I was the one who paid it. He forwarded the money to me in this instance, but if you are in a domestic violence situation, that may not necessarily happen. My insurance company's policy didn't consider that. If they understood the mindset of an abuser, they might see that if he is in a good mood, he might pay his spouse the reimbursement money, but there would be no guarantee that he would, and the woman might be out money that she may desperately need for her child. There is a hole in this policy that needs fixing. It could be changed. I'm passionate about fixing things like that and lots more.

Today I have a life filled with joy and abundance. I am modeling how to live for those who have been hurt and, more importantly for those who have hurt me. They are the ones that are stuck in fear and negativity, and I would love for them to see my example and turn their lives around too.

For women who have been abused, my advice is to find people who you are emotionally safe with like Susan and her Thriver Community. They will be the allies and friends who will not judge but support you. They will inspire you to follow your passions and live your dreams. That has been my journey, and I wish you well on yours.

I am a thriver, and living well is my best revenge!

— *Cathryn*

~ ~ ~ ~ ~ ~ ~ ~ ~ ~ ~ ~ ~ ~ ~ ~

Every day I write my name in stars
across the Universe. I am love.
The power of my flame rises
with the fury of my dreams.

— NANCY WOOD

THRIVER SUCCESS STORIES

Jenny

*Courage starts with showing up
and letting ourselves be seen.*
— Brené Brown

FROM THE BEGINNING

The one thing I remember about coming to Susan's workshop was how I was struggling with the symptoms of Post-Traumatic Stress Disorder (PTSD) at the time. I was hypervigilant, constantly feeling like something bad was about to happen to me, and I had trouble sleeping. I was really anxious. I was functioning, though, so every therapist I went told me, "Oh! You're fine." But I didn't feel fine, and I didn't want to live like this anymore. It was one of the darkest times I ever remember living through.

I wasn't suicidal. I didn't want to end my life, but every morning, I didn't want to get up and face another day. The thought of having to exist for one more day and get through it was more than I could handle. I was exhausted just thinking about it. If I had gone to bed and not woken up, I think I would have been okay with that at that time just because it seemed like a better alternative. I didn't think I was strong enough to get through and feel like this. I was in an almost hopeless place.

When I did try to face the day ahead of me, I had fits of obsessive, compulsive cleaning and then outbursts that made controlling my emotions difficult. I would get so upset and then have a really hard time cycling down. My parents didn't know what to do with me. Their advice to me for coping with the abuse in my marriage was: "Let it go; don't say anything; don't rock the boat." Sure, that's how I was raised, but suddenly that advice had gotten me into a really bad situation, and it wasn't working for me. I couldn't keep things bottled in anymore. I didn't want to feel like I had to be ashamed. I had taken plenty, and I was done.

In order to find a way to cope with what I was experiencing, I looked for a support group, a place I could find other people who had survived domestic violence to help me. I had to figure out a way to get back to feeling normal again. That was my goal. I just wanted to feel like a normal person. I didn't want to feel like this anymore. I remember that very clearly. That was the goal.

I googled "support groups for domestic violence survivors" or something like that, and a workshop came up through the Hartford Health Care network. I was working there at the time, and the workshop was free, so I thought I had nothing to lose. It was on the weekend which was good and really convenient for me because I didn't have commitments at the time except for work. I would say that one of the big things for me was it didn't cost me anything, although if there had been a fee, I probably would have paid it. But financial abuse is usually associated with mental abuse in domestic violence situations, so it could be hard for some women to get access to a workshop program like this if there had been a fee.

A WAY OUT

I remember coming to the workshop and finding that there were some other women in the workshop who had come through abuse and had been in Susan's program for a while. I could see that they were in a different place in their lives, and for me that felt like here I could find a way out of this. Not only were they showing me that there was a way to get to a different place, but also hearing the other women talk, it was so clear to me that they did not bring this abuse upon themselves. This was not their fault. If you can accept that about someone else, it makes it a lot easier to accept it about yourself.

I needed to hear that because one of the therapists I had seen about my abusive situation told me, "You understand that this is all your fault, right?" I was not in a place to hear that. She didn't say it bluntly like that, but that was basically what I heard from her. I think what she was trying to convey to me is that it would be really helpful if someone like me who had been raised as a "people pleaser" and had been in an abusive relationship could identify that as a problem and work on it. But I was not at that place yet. I was still putting the pieces back together and building myself back up again. I was a shattered person, and when you are shattered like that, it isn't helpful having someone tell you that this is essentially your fault and you could prevent this from happening to you again if you worked on yourself a little. I was definitely not ready for that yet.

One of the first things I remember doing in Susan's workshop was decorating a journal while quiet music was playing. That was a nice way to step out of myself and into a place where I could be creative. It was a great way to start things, and it helped make the workshop a safe place to be emotional. I still wasn't comfortable processing my experience there in that way yet, but it wasn't safe for me for me to process it emotionally in front of my parents, and I didn't have a close network of friends at that time to lean on. So Susan's workshop and the writing we did there became the first safe, supportive place where I could be and process what I was going through.

THE HAPPY PERSON INSIDE

Here's one of the pieces I wrote in a writing exercise at the workshop was for *Step Three: Connect with the Happy Person Inside You,* of Susan's *Seven Steps to Thriving After Abuse.* It is a letter to me from my Happy Person Inside.

Dear Jenny,

I am the Happy Person inside You and I want you to tell you something. I want you to be empowered by your past and find a way to use your experience to help other women. I want you to get back to doing things you love like painting, gardening and working on your house. I want you to let go of worrying and get back to living life. Get back to seeing the world and experiencing all life has to offer. I want you to ignore things people say to "help" when they make you feel badly. I want you to stop trying to live up to anyone's expectations other than your own. I want you to know that you can still be caring and thoughtful AND stand up for yourself. I want you to accept that your mother doesn't always know what's best for you. I want you to realize and finally believe in your heart that the people who abused you and treated you unfairly were the problem – not you. You didn't deserve the things that were said and done to you.

You are a loving, capable and independent person. The things you have been through do not take away from the person you were, are and will be. You are not worthless because you were abused. You are healthy. You are strong. You are someone other people can look up to. You are someone your parents can be proud of. You have the ability to live a great life. You have the power to achieve your dreams. You can do anything you set your mind to. You will not be held back by fear. You will not be overwhelmed by life. You will sleep at night. You will not have nightmares anymore. You will live your life however you choose, and it will be a great one. You will make a positive impact on the world. It won't happen overnight, but it will happen. You will find a happy place. You will feel safe again.

Reconnecting with my Happy Person Inside, who had such wisdom and encouragement for me, was very emotional. I remember crying while I read this piece above to the women in the workshop, but everyone was so supportive. Susan told me to see the tears as a release, and they were.

After I finished the first Saturday of the two-day workshop, I started emailing Susan my writing and poems. I think you forget about parts of yourself when you go through a bad time, and oh yeah! I forgot that I used to write. In high school, I was in advanced English classes and got good feedback on my writing. I also found journaling to be very therapeutic for me and helpful particularly when I traveled because I wanted to remember my experiences. Suddenly, writing in the workshop got me back into writing as a tool for healing and expression.

Living in an abusive relationship, you learn how to become so small. Coming out of it is doing the opposite. It is giving yourself permission to use your voice, take up space, be creative and let your whole self out. You don't have to hide parts of yourself anymore or diminish yourself to make other people more comfortable.

Here are some of the pieces I sent to Susan in the week between the first and second sessions of her workshop. I was on fire with my writing!

Sometimes

by Jenny

*Sometimes a woman needs to get angry
With injustice in the world.*

*Sometimes a quiet woman needs to speak up
To defend someone she cares about.*

*Sometimes a meek woman needs to be strong
And set an example for others.*

*Sometimes a sad woman needs to be happy
To remind herself she can be.*

*Sometimes a peaceful woman needs to fight
Because she knows what she believes in.*

Why Me

by Jenny

*Some people ask, "Why me?"
I say, "Why not me?"
Why shouldn't I achieve my dreams?
What is holding me back, really?
If other people can achieve success and happiness,
Why not me?
I am capable of creating opportunities.
I am resourceful and committed.
I am no less deserving or able bodied.
Why not me?
What do I have to lose other than fear?*

My Addiction

by Jenny

I have an addiction.
The doctors think it isn't good for me,
But I won't listen.
I won't give it up.
I will push myself to the limit.
I want to feel the rush.
My addiction is running.

RUNNING AS MY GOAL

Coming out of Susan's workshop, running was something else that I had enjoyed doing since high school, and like the writing I had forgotten I used to love to do, running was also a tremendous release for me.

I had run on and off when I was in that abusive relationship. Running has always been for me an expression of freedom. It gives you a break from what you are dealing with and gets you out of your head. Running has always been a meditative experience for me even before I realized that that was why I was doing it. But after you go through something really awful and traumatic that brings you a new low, running longer distances shifts your perspective to a different kind of challenge to overcome. So when I would go running and hit a spot that felt really hard, I'd think, This is worse than being in an abusive relationship, and this isn't that hard. I can do it.

Maybe it was the abuse I experienced that gave me the fuel to run these longer distances and to do things that were really difficult for me, because they were not as difficult as what I had already survived. I feel like that might be the same for people who have been through cancer or struggled with addiction. They get into running really long distances, too, because such a challenge can reaffirm to you that you can do hard things. Life is going to be hard sometimes, but you can handle it.

QUIETING THE INNER CRITIC

Another helpful exercise in Susan's workshop was in *Step Two: Quiet the Inner Critic*. I leaned how important it was for me to acknowledge that I had an inner negative voice and to identify where that voice was coming from. When you hear it, you can wonder if it is your own internal dialogue. *Am I still running the loops on my ex or my mother's insecurities having been raised by her? Is that voice really something that I am thinking or did I pick that up from someplace else? Is it really relevant to what's going in my life right now?*

Here's another poem I sent to Susan after the workshop

Letting Go

by Jenny

Today I am letting go.

I am lightening my load.

I am accepting my many imperfections.

I am learning to love myself.

I am spreading my wings. I am taking flight!

And I'm taking you with me. We are healing.

We are renewing our beauty from the inside out.

I don't even remember writing this, but it feels like a piece that describes how the Happy Person Inside You is overcoming the kind of fear and limiting beliefs you may have about yourself or your Inner Beauty while the Inner Critic is playing back the more negative part of your past experiences over and over in your head like a broken record.

I know that my Inner Critic feeds the fear that holds me back by replaying what I was told as a child. There thoughts were instilled in me like "Don't try that! You could fail!" I was told, "If you aren't good at something, why continue to do it when you are so awful at it?" Why couldn't I just enjoy doing something I know I'm not good at but really like doing?

You carry these negative thoughts that your parents probably got from their parents, and it's like one big, negative cycle from one generation to another. I can see how my mom, who lived in this very small world with a critical mother, could have developed a super loud Inner Critic that then was channeled into the rest of us. Now I'm breaking that cycle and letting go of other people's expectations as well as any fear that is holding me back. I have to, as the poem suggests, lighten my load and not be weighed down by other people's stuff.

SETTING NEW GOALS

Coming out of Susan's workshop with the final step being *Step Seven: Set New Goals,* I signed up for and ran a 10K race. Halfway through I thought I was going to die, but I had to keep going. I figured that if I could do a 10K and halfway through felt like I was going to die, I could sign and run a half marathon pretty easily. I was so proud when I did a ten-mile race, and then I signed up for a half marathon. In the half marathon training, I was actually running longer than a half marathon. So I signed up for a marathon training, and that's when I contacted Susan about doing fundraising for the nonprofit organization that supports Susan's workshops so that they are provided to the women free of charge. After I did the Hartford Marathon, I started running ultras. I would also do a big race every fall as a fundraiser for Domestic Violence Awareness Month, which I called *Running for the Color Purple.* Purple is the color identified with domestic violence awareness.

During that time period, I also started blogging as *The Running Thriver* to document my journey as a runner and as a woman on the journey from victim to survivor to thriver. I continued writing that blog for several years as well as running more and more races and challenges.

WHAT IS A THRIVER?

What a thriver meant to me when I first attended the workshop and what being a thriver means to me now are two very different things. At first, being a thriver was about living in the moment, letting go of what had happened to me in my past and living without fear. Now I feel that thriving is really about living authentically and letting go of the feeling that you have to please people or worry about how other people feel about you. While I want people to be comfortable being with me, I feel that now my need to please is within reason. Before I was afraid to have people come to my house – a fixer-upper – because it wasn't the way I wanted it to be. I was concerned about what people might think of me. Now I can say, "This is who I am. This is my life! It is what it is. I will make you feel welcome, but I'm not going to go crazy cleaning my house from top to bottom and scrubbing it down, because I have two kids and two dogs. This is how we live!" If that makes you uncomfortable, then you are not my people. I've been looking for a tribe of people in my life who accept me for who I am instead of trying to fit myself to belong in places I don't really want to be anymore.

A WORK IN PROGRESS

Today, for the first time in my life, I am someone who is very comfortable in her own skin. I am good with who I am, but I accept that I am, like most people, a work in progress. I know where I want to be in life, and right now, not everything is where I want it to be, but I do have a game plan. I don't feel like it all needs to be figured out right now, and that has been a huge mental shift for me. In the past year or two, I have been growing a lot into myself, becoming more self-aware, being more in touch with what I really want instead what I feel like society is expecting me to want. Looking at my career, in which I have invested a lot of time and energy, I feel that it's okay if I don't want to do that forever, to pursue something else even if I don't have as much financial security. That was a hard thing to wrap my head around.

I feel if you can accept yourself and where you are at, then you can take things for what they are and not ascribe extra meaning to them. You don't have to feel you are a failure because you didn't get your kids to eat three meals that day or go to bed on time. Some days are better than others, and those days you're going to cruise through, whereas other days are going to be really difficult. That's just how life is!

PLANNING AHEAD

My life plan post-abuse was that I was going to buy my own house, which I did, and when I was ready, if I had the urge to have children, I was going to adopt them.

Part Four

I didn't even factor a man into the equation. I told my mother that the only way I was going to get involved in another relationship was with somebody who absolutely loved and adored me. That was my criteria.

I met Adam through an online dating service, although I had already cancelled my membership because I had decided it was not for me and that I wasn't ready. The idea of dating made me feel a little panicked. But he contacted me, and told me that he lived in my town and had a dog. So I figured that he couldn't be that awful of a person if he could keep a pet. He said he was just looking for someone to spend time with because he was living with a couple of guys in a house they were renting, but he worked a different shift than his roommates. I only worked three days a week because I worked very long shifts, so he was looking for someone to go do stuff with. The first time we met up, we went hiking with our dogs because obviously I still didn't totally trust going out alone with a guy. So I brought my dog and he brought his dog. We hiked at Sleeping Giant and had a very pleasant time. When I got home, he called me and asked me if I wanted to go to a movie, and after that we started to hang out regularly.

I had just moved into my house, and my dogs were having trouble adjusting. One of them was keeping me up all night barking because of the strange noises. So Adam started coming there during the day while I was at work, and he would wear my dogs out so that they would let me sleep at night. He'd also fix all the stuff in my house that needed fixing. Owning an old house, there were a lot of things to be repaired. So he'd fix cabinet doors so that they would close easily, and I would leave him snacks.

On a Memorial Day weekend, I invited him to a picnic with my family because I knew he didn't have family close by, and he came and spent the day with my family. My mother said, "If he'll come to spend the day with your family, he likes you as more than a friend." So that's how we ended up in a relationship. Because he flew under the radar, and we were hanging out low-pressure for a long time before we started dating.

A NEW, HEALTHY RELATIONSHIP

With Adam, I had come from this idea that relationships were work, and all relationships were hard. But it is hard to not get along with Adam, and it's hard to stay mad at him. It was the easiest thing to fall to love with him because he is such an agreeable person. He puts everyone first and has the biggest heart. He would bend over backward for anyone and give them the shirt off his back and not think twice about it. This is not someone who was ever going to willfully cause me pain because it would tear him up inside. Yes, being in a relationship with him has been work, and we have times where we've had to go off and both work on ourselves. But we have always found our way back to each other.

I hadn't really thought about what a healthy relationship with someone would look like. I didn't have any role models growing up for what such a healthy relationship would look like. But Adam's parents do have a very respectful relationship and so do his aunt and uncle. I love his mom and his aunt, and they are great role models for me. When I go to his aunt's house, it feels like coming home to me. I tell her that's what I want – for my house to feel like home when people come to visit. I want to be able to say, "Make yourself at home. You are welcome here. Get comfortable."

BECOMING A MOTHER

Being a mother is challenging no matter how well equipped you are or how good your support system is. Your kids are just going to challenge you in ways that no one else can and make you question every decision you make. My parenting philosophy is accepting that there are times when I am going to screw things up and lose my temper. I am human, but I own it and apologize to my kids when I have messed up and hold them accountable when they need to own their behavior.

I work on making sure that they always feel loved because I can remember that growing up, I was a difficult kid. I was a lot like my daughter, really stubborn and had a mind of my own. I can remember not wanting to listen to my mother because I didn't feel loved by her. Instead I felt resented, but there was so much more going on that I didn't understand between my mom and dad. In my family at home, I was always labeled the bad kid, the out-of-control kid, the kid with behavioral issues. But when I went to a friend's houses or at school, everyone thought I was an awesome kid. It wasn't until I went to college that I understood that I was not the problem; I just grew up in a very dysfunctional environment. A lot of the anxiety I had as a kid went away when I went to college. It was like a breath of fresh air for me at school, but then I'd go home for holidays and I'd be bouncing around inside because the volume of the environment around me was up too high. I am very much the receiver of energy. As an adult, I have learned how to set boundaries, a lesson learned so much later in life.

I try to keep all of this in mind with my kids today, like when my daughter is pushing all of my buttons. I have to ask, "Is there something wrong or do you just need Mommy's attention?" And nine times out of ten, she'll say, "I need cuddles," and that's the end of it. Kids use the skills that they have when you are busy doing something and they want your attention.

GETTING BACK TO RUNNING

Recently I ran my first marathon after having my two kids. That was crazy and very emotional because I had to give myself space to get back to training and doing things for me. Once you become a mother, you can go weeks and weeks and weeks without ever doing something for yourself. You start to wonder why you feel so wound up and stressed all the time, and then you realize that you can't remember a time that you did a single thing for yourself. It's the polar opposite of being single where you only have to worry about yourself. I had to give myself permission to take time for myself. I had to say to my husband, "Adam, it's all you! You have got this! I'm leaving. I'm going to the gym, doing my thing." He was super supportive. Men need to be asked. They are not going to offer. As women, we expect men to offer because we offer, but that's not how they are wired.

In the process of training for that marathon, I got back to ultra-running and did two 50Ks, which was amazing. That was my little secret heart desire. I wanted to get back to ultrarunning, but training two to five hours a week would be insane for me. So I was super pumped that I could put in almost no training and still run an ultra. Running an ultra is running a distance longer than a marathon. So I ran two separate 50Ks, which is like thirty-one-plus miles. I was super over the moon about that. The first 50K was the end of June last year. The second one was in September. Then I did a marathon after that.

I also have goals about my career. Doing what I am doing now is not what I want to do forever, and I find that the people I gravitate toward are people who have their own business. I do have my personal trainer's certification, and I have been working on a counseling certification. Once my kids are a little older, my end goal would be scale back on my medical Physician's Assistant (PA) role and do more personal training/life coaching/counseling work. I would like to build up my own practice, and I've been thinking a lot about getting back into writing because I haven't written on my blog (*The Running Thriver*) in a long time. I want to get back into the habit of writing by blogging about life as a mom and an ultra-runner and how those two things are not that different. They are both about running on empty and doing things that your body doesn't want to do! Eventually I want to write a book and maybe start a podcast. I would be doing the kind of things that people I admire do.

A LIFE OF POWER AND PURPOSE

Having a life of power and purpose as a thriver is a lot of trial and error, but in order to find things that resonate with you, you have to be open and looking for them. That's harder when you are stuck in what society expects you to do. For example, I spent a lot of money on my education, and I have a really good career. People would consider me successful. But what if what you are doing no longer feels fulfilling? You have to ask yourself what kinds of things make you feel excited. I know I get excited when I see my friend who is a photographer posting stuff about her business growing. I get excited when I'm listening to The Same 24 Hours, one of my favorite author's podcast. She went from a career as a real successful lawyer to now being a writer, hosting a podcast and coaching athletes. She is on a journey of self-discovery, and I feel like that's what I should be doing now in my life. I should be discovering who I want to be, what I want to do and how to get there.

I have been reading a lot of Brené Brown (author of *Daring Greatly* and other books and TED Talks). She talks about having the courage to be authentic and says things like:

"Listen! This is Me! This is my sometimes-messy life. These are the things that I really struggle with and others that I have always been good at."

I've learned that It's okay to put it all out there like that. Because If I am really okay with who I am and I'm comfortable saying so, then I am opening the door for someone else to say what they think about it too. I don't think people realize how heavy it is to carry around all of those expectations and caring about what other people think. But you don't need to carry that. Your people are out there, and it is more important to find where you belong than to be liked.

Listening to Brené Brown speak and how she battles with her Inner Critic, I can see how the stuff she puts out there is affecting so many people. Can you imagine if she listened to her Inner Critic and the people who criticize her? She would shrink down and wouldn't share any of it. When I first started blogging as *The Running Thriver*, I'd get that kind of critical comment and it used to kill me. I felt like I would never write a book because I don't have the thick skin to take the criticism. I would think, *I don't want to take this to the next level, because I don't want that much attention and I can't handle the feedback.* Now I'm at a point in my life where I can see that this could get really uncomfortable, but you can take it or leave it and you are not going to please everyone. The potential of being able to really help and connect with somebody is worth the risk of that others will say something negative because they are unhappy with their own lives.

LIVING WELL

The quote "Living well is best revenge" is the starting point of the journey after abuse because you'll eventually get to a place where you don't need to avenge the abuse anymore. Eventually when you see the abuse was something that happened to you, you will learn from it and then you go on with your life. Not that what happened to me doesn't still affect me. There are times during the year that catch me off guard. I find myself being irritable and wound up, and then I remember that I'm in that part of the year when it got really tumultuous for me and my body still reacts to it to this day. But within the past year I've reached the point that I don't hope anything bad happens anymore to my ex-husband who was abusive to me. I'm over the karma thing. Hurt people hurt people. I'm not in a place where I'm hurting anymore. I hope that he got help and that he's in a better place, and I hope he is a better person.

I'm okay with what happened to me. It showed me that I was a lot stronger than I ever thought I was. It broke me of being a people pleaser, and it has helped me connect with people. So "living well is the best revenge" got me through the first ten years, but now I don't need it anymore. I totally clung to the idea in the beginning that I wanted the revenge to be against my ex-husband. I sold my wedding rings, and I bought a bike. I think that was about him saying to me that I couldn't handle any little thing. My response was I'll show him what I can't handle! So I signed up and trained for an Iron Man, not knowing how to bike or swim. I was going to show him. But now I'm at a point that I don't care what he thinks. I don't care of what people think of me in general. I'm good with who I am. I do not have any contact with him, but I'm also through looking to see if he has been arrested online. I'd really rather see that he gets help.

I see that the person I was at the time was doing the best she could. She was not in a great place. She didn't have the best coping skills. She came from a dysfunctional background. I think I am in a good place right now. I don't wish her revenge.

Instead, I need more compassion for who I used to be. And to some degree, I even have compassion for my ex-husband because what kind of life do you have if that is how you treat other people? How happy can you be? How much can you accomplish in life if you are blaming all of your problems on everyone else? You can't fix a problem if you aren't being accountable for it.

I am amazed at how far I have come in the ten years since meeting Susan. I am grateful for the journey and where I am now. But her workshop only opens the door. You go to a workshop and someone opens the door and there is the path to a more fulfilling life. It's up to you to walk through the door and do the work. But then, before you went to the workshop, maybe you couldn't find the door.

I am a thriver! Living well is my best revenge!

— *Jenny*

~~~~~~~~~~~~~~~~~

Because true belonging only happens when we present our authentic, imperfect selves to the world, our sense of belonging can never be greater than our level of self-acceptance.

— BRENÉ BROWN

Part Four

THRIVER SUCCESS STORIES

Pamela

The day you were born a ladder was set up
to help you escape from this world.

— RUMI

FROM THE BEGINNING

When I first came to one of Susan's workshop in February 2013, I didn't see any future ahead of me. I was totally inside myself, barely speaking to anyone, not just in the workshop but in my life in general. I had no dreams about what I wanted to be in my life. I had a tiny bit of hope, but not a lot. Hope means to me that something good is coming and you can start to see that there are possibilities out there. But I had little hope.

At that time, I was married to a man who believed that everything I did I was wrong. I would try to fix things, but he still would say they were all wrong. I lost all my belief in myself. I am a very smart person, but I felt like a really stupid person. Why can't I get the budget? I was married to him for twenty-four years, and every day I did something else wrong. I thought I was a bad person and my husband was just reacting to how bad I was.

All of this affected me. I was withdrawn, stayed away from my friends and had low self-esteem. In fact, I barely had any at all. One day someone wrote me a note with a name and phone number on it. It took me three months to call the number and when I did, it was the local domestic violence shelter. I reached out for help and went there in secret to see a counselor. I was deathly afraid of being found out by my husband.

When I was there, I was given a flyer for Susan's workshop. I thought the workshop would be good to go to, but it took several more months for me to attend a workshop session because I had to make up where I was going so I wouldn't be found out.

But I did have this drive to get out of the marriage and get my children out of the house. I think I would have left a lot earlier if I had seen what he was doing to me, but I couldn't live with what he was doing to my kids.

IMAGINING A FUTURE

When I came into Susan's workshop, I didn't know what to expect. By then, I was dissociating with Post Traumatic Stress Syndrome (PTSD) and had been in individual therapy for a couple of years as well as in marriage counseling with my husband. I knew that sometimes when you are in situations like this, you get into a group where people complain about all these horrible things that they have been through. What struck me about Susan's workshop was that it wasn't about those horrible things. Instead, Susan wanted us to focus on what good things were coming around the corner. It started me thinking that maybe there are some other options out there for me, not just for everyone else and all the other women in that workshop. I was thinking maybe I had a future after all.

MOST HELPFUL EXERCISES

When Susan began her workshop with *Step One: See Your Journey from her Seven Steps to Thriving After Abuse,* I was asked to pick out a fairy tale to write about for the exercise. I immediately said Cinderella. I always felt a connection to her because of the animals and how she talked to them. But Susan helped me see how Cinderella transformed by the end of the story. Susan said that Cinderella found her happy ending with the prince by completing herself as a person first and finding a complete person in the prince. Susan's telling of the story surprised me because I always thought of myself as a bad person and that nothing good would ever happen to me. Susan talked about Cinderella's movement from struggle to transformation to happy ending as a journey.

When she wrote on the board "VICTIM to SURVIVOR to THRIVER" to describe the journey we were on as victims of domestic violence, I knew right then that my goal was to be a thriver. I did see myself then a survivor, even although I was still in an abusive relationship, but Susan gave me the idea that there was something more I could focus on as a thriver. While the women in the workshop really impressed me with their visions for the future, I didn't have much to say about my future because I was still really inside myself and withdrawn. At that time, I had this idea that when you are born, you pick who you are going to be and what kind of life you were going to have. I believed that I was put on this earth just to suffer and get through it.

When we did the exercise in *Step Two: Quiet the Inner Critic* of Susan's *Seven Steps to Thriving After Abuse*, I thought, *What am I telling myself? Was it my Inner Critic and not me that was saying all that negative stuff about me?* I knew everyone had a good side and a bad side, but because of my upbringing and the relationship I was in at the time, I thought everything about me was bad. Sure, I had to help people around me, but I would never have anything. I'd never get beyond the suffering. But Susan and the other women in the workshop challenged all that. I loved that the women were open and loving, with warm personalities. They were so comfortable in their skins, and that's something I wanted to have. I want to be authentic and find out who I really am.

WHAT IS A THRIVER?

Before I came to the workshop, I thought a thriver was someone who had it all together. She was rich, really warm, taking good care of her kids and had every quality you would ever want. Now I think of a thriver as somebody who takes whatever their life gives them – a lot of people have bad things going on – and they just walk through it. They are able to be kind to people along the way, pursue their goals and keep going and trying.

Today I can see that I'm getting there as a thriver. I have grown a lot, and I've been trying different things. Recently I sat myself down and had a chat with myself because I have been struggling to get a teaching job that pays well. I love teaching, but I don't love it so much to give up my whole life for it. In my last teaching job, I worked almost 24/7 to get all the planning, homework and paperwork done. One of my daughters has special needs, and the other is in college. If I am totally drained in a teaching job, I don't have time for them. That made me realize that I want to devote a lot of more time to my family and be more present in my daughters' lives. Maybe teaching was not the job for me.

So I applied for four jobs and got interviewed for all of them the next day. Now these jobs are bringing in some money, and the rest of the time I can be with my kids. I found another way to work with kids which I love at a natural day care, and I'm loving it.

Best of all, I learned that if I'm in a job that's not working for me, I'm out of there right away and looking for another job. Ten years ago, I would have stayed there and not taken care of myself. No more!

WHO I WANT TO BE

In Susan's follow-up group for the women who complete her two-day workshop, I like it when Susan gives us some questions or "writing prompts" to write about. Some of them turn out to very deep, but only after you think about them for a while – like my idea of that a thriver is not someone who is perfect. She is someone who is able to deal with things, and it doesn't matter if she deals with them perfectly or not. She does it, and she gets through it. A thriver finds joy in her life and gives hope to others. I think you can be the poorest person, but you can still give another person an extra pair of socks!

With my new perception of what a thriver is, I no longer think I am worthless. I am worth something. Like the other women who have gone through what I have and have achieved greatness as a thriver, there is a possibility that I could do that too. I'm so creative and musical. Lately, I found out there are other people who are like me and it's okay to do the things I love to do. I definitely have joy in my life now, lots of joy. My kids give me joy. I enjoy the women's groups that I attend, and when I work with kids that gives me joy. Kids are so honest and come up with such wonderful things. They don't have those filters or fears, like "Oh! I can't say that or they'll think I'm bad." They just go for it.

When I was five, I was a very happy kid. I told people what to do. One day, I wanted to go to swing at the playground at the school. So I walked there. It was a mile away. At some point, I was missed and apparently the whole neighbor was out looking for me. But I knew exactly where I was, and I was swinging on that swing because that's what I wanted to do, and I was happy.

I want to be that person again. I didn't have fears of other people then. I want to unlearn all those things that made me shut down. I want to find my true self again in that kid who decided that she wanted to do something that made her feel good and gave her joy and she figured out how to do it. I want to put myself back where I was when I was five years old.

LIVING WELL

I am on the road to living well because now I'm focused on how I am living and what I want out of life. I can decide what kind of person I want to be, what I want to do and what kind of relationships I want to have. My biggest dream is to write books for children that would help them notice that something may not be right in their homes. When they do figure it out, then they can offhandedly say something to a friend or a teacher or an adult without it being really obvious and get the help they need.

I'd like to do picture books with different characters and have each book dealing with a different issue. The book would tell the kids what shouldn't happen in their homes or at school. I have already written a story about a girl with low self-esteem who gets bullied.

My vision for my life today is to take the talents and skills I have and combine them into a career – a business that can help children or adults by showing them how they can make a change in their lives. I'd like to be a working artist, creating books for children and working every day, like in a painting workshop. This would make me happy and bring me great joy.

I am a thriver! Living well is my best revenge!

– Pamela

I am a Woman of Power

by Pamela

I am a woman of power.
I am enough!
I am a woman of power.
I love myself!
I am a woman of power.

I am me!
I am a woman of power.
I protect myself!
I am a woman of power.
I am independent!
I am a woman of power.
I take care of myself!
I am a woman of power.
I am loved!
I am a woman of power.
I feel my feelings!
I am a woman of power.
I am creative!
I am a woman of power.
I can and I will!
I am a woman of power.
I rise again!!

~ ~ ~ ~ ~ ~ ~ ~ ~ ~ ~ ~ ~ ~ ~

Develop enough courage so that you can stand up for yourself and then stand up for somebody else.

— MAYA ANGELOU

Part Four

THRIVER SUCCESS STORIES

Sophia

The ability to triumph begins with you. Always.
— Oprah Winfrey

FROM THE BEGINNING

I first came into one of Susan's workshops in January of 2004. It was a cold winter day outside, and I was going through something that I kept telling myself never should have happened to me. I was broken. As I walked around the corner to the room where the workshop was being held, I felt like I was going to a place of refuge. It was going to be someplace better than where I was, and someone there was going to educate me about what I was experiencing. It was an intervention, and I needed it. I needed someone to tell me that I deserved better and that things would get better with the information I was about to receive.

As I hobbled into the room on crutches due to the fractured knee I had from a domestic violence incident, I met Susan and she asked me my name. I told her, but she asked me to repeat it because she wasn't able to hear what I said. My voice was so soft, barely above a whisper. I was feeling weak, like all my power had been taken away from me by what had happened. Then, too, I was entering a new environment, a room full of strangers, and I felt vulnerable. They say domestic violence is a silent violence, but now these people would know something about me, something bad. I felt shame and guilt.

I don't remember if I told my story that day. Susan doesn't usually have us tell our stories when we first come into the workshop. But if I said anything, it was probably something brief to explain the brace on my leg. But I was motivated to come to the workshop. I saw it as a sign that I should attend because I had just found out about the

Saturday session earlier that same week when I went to the domestic violence shelter in my town. It was a Tuesday night, and a flyer on the bulletin board at the shelter announced that Susan's workshop was at the end of that week. I needed a resource like that. There was an urgency for me to get help me and get out of this situation I was in. I knew I wanted a better life, but I'm not sure in that moment I was thinking that my future would get any better. All I knew was that maybe I'd learn something in that workshop that would give me the strength and self-determination to make a decision about where my life was going.

MY UNCERTAIN FUTURE

I was most uncertain about what would happen next for me because at that time I was a member of a church and so was my husband. The church was aware of what had occurred between us, and they were going to work with me about the situation. But I wondered about what kind of conversation they were going to have with me and how I would respond. Would they try to influence me to stay in the relationship? In the end, the church was very respectful of where I was, and they left it up to me to make the decision. They never forced me to go back. I felt that for them, safety came first. Still I was unsure what I wanted to do.

My husband and I had recently purchased a home – a house because you make a house a home – and we had everything we had ever wanted, our part of the American Dream. How could we make this right and maintain a healthy relationship? I was faced with so many other questions. How do I tell my children? What do I say to my family and the others in my life? Would they judge me about the decision I was going to make about my relationship?

In the end, what I decided was very supported by the church and by the women in Susan's Thriver Community. I trusted God to help me make my own decision about my safety and what was best for me and my family. Initially, I did stay in the relationship, and for a time with the support of our church and my support network, things were better between us. But eventually old behaviors reemerged, and I did leave the marriage and get divorced. Through all that time, though, I kept coming to Susan's follow-up sessions and activities. I told myself that I needed to keep remembering what had happened to me and how I wanted to be in a healthy relationship.

ANSWERING THE CALL

In the workshop, Susan helped me answer the call and begin my journey from victim to survivor to thriver. I was sure that I no longer wanted domestic violence to be the norm in my life, and I knew that life was not a destination but a journey. I found the help I needed in Susan's Thriver Community to take that journey and move forward with my life. I had never heard about being a "thriver" before I met Susan, and with that new word, I knew it was the place where I wanted to be. Hearing the word thriver repeatedly in Susan's group embedded the idea in my mind and heart that being a thriver means you are moving forward and going places! I wanted to show everyone around me what being a thriver looked like.

MOST HELPFUL EXERCISES

One of Susan's exercises that really helped me was to create my own *I Am a Woman of Power* statement. Here's what I wrote in 2004 when I first came to a workshop.

I am a woman of power who has made a positive impact on the world through my own healing, wellness and creativity.

I am a woman of power who has integrity and always believes in doing the right thing, even when it is challenging. It exposes my true character when no one sees me but God.

I am a woman of power who has embarked upon this earth to make a difference in other women's lives, to inspire them to achieve their highest level of humanity and cultivate the world with love.

Today I celebrate my life by being true to myself, being open to others and being filled with positive energy. This transformation has brought out the best in me, taught me self-love and, like a flower bud, allowed me to blossom into a beautiful rose.

Today I celebrate my life, which resembles the ever-changing four seasons – fall to winter, winter to spring, and then spring to summer – secure that I can go forward with confidence and without fear of anything.

– Sophia

The word *power* is profound to me. I have power, and I will not give my power away to anyone. I am not powerless. I am powerful.

Another helpful exercise was *Step Three: Connect with the Happy Person Inside You.* Writing a letter to myself from the Happy Person Inside allowed me to reconnect with what makes me happy. Oftentimes we, particularly as women, are so busy making other people happy that we forget about what makes us happy. It can be so simple. For me, being happy is about peace. It is about joy. It is about protecting my power. It was in Susan's workshop that I realized that I had lost my power and needed to get it back. But I didn't want the kind of power when someone takes control over another person. I'm talking about "shared" power in a relationship where I am able to do what I need to do, and who I am is recognized and supported by my partner. Living a life that is empowering is what thriving is all about.

MY THRIVER ROLE MODEL

Oprah Winfrey is one of my "thriver" role models. Having the opportunity to meet her several years ago was a dream come true for me. I won the "Live Your Best Life Ever Spa Week" contest in 2008 along with fifty other women and spent a week with Oprah and Gayle King at a spa in Arizona. It is still surreal for me to think that really did happen. It was also amazing how I manifested that dream because of positive thoughts and support of Susan's Thriver Community. Susan teaches her motivational model for manifesting a desire in her workshops, and it is included in her *Staying in the Thriver Zone: A Road Map to Manifesting a Life of Power and Purpose,* the second book in *The Thriver Zone Series*™.

It was at one of the annual retreat weekends for Susan's Thriver Community that I put the model to the test. At that October 2007 retreat, we did skits in which we imagined we were on Oprah's television talk show. Several of us played Oprah that day, including me, and I was excited. I had been drawn to Oprah and her positive energy from the first time I saw her on television when I was in high school. There was something so empowering for me about her. A few months after the retreat, I got an email late one night about a contest and I filled out the application online. I didn't think about it much until I got a phone call in February that I had won. By March of that same year, my meeting with Oprah had become a reality.

For me, the way I manifested an opportunity to meet Oprah brings me back to my faith. My spirituality has taught me that if you speak it, God hears it and you will be given the desire of your heart. That's what manifesting is all about.

What I also have learned from Oprah is that "Luck is preparation meeting opportunity." Oprah says that her success in life has not been just good luck. More often, she says when opportunities presented themselves in her life, she was prepared to go to the next level. I feel, like Oprah, I have been preparing for what comes next in my life for a while now. Being a part of the Susan's Thriver Community has equipped me with the information and support I need to move forward and thrive after the abuse. Like a diamond being refined, I have been chipping away the rough stuff I have experienced, and with fifteen years of thriving behind me as part of Susan's community, I am prepared to move forward as a thriver.

WHAT IS A THRIVER?

To me, being a thriver is about movement. It is about processing our experiences in life, the good as well as the difficult ones and doing self-reflection so that we can move on to that next level of self-improvement. Just as I have been inspired by those, like Susan, who have been empowered by the tragedy they have faced, I know that I, too, can be a role model for others by moving beyond the circumstances of my life. I have something I can give back to people who are hurting. We all have something that has caused us pain and trauma and giving back once we move beyond that pain and trauma is our legacy of hope to others. What has helped me most in moving from survivor to thriver has been having access to the right resources. There were things I needed to thrive going forward, like educational opportunities, jobs, housing, financial literacy and transportation. Having access to all of that and more means we can shape who we become, and it allow us to believe that we deserve it. We have to get out of a negative mindset and go step-by-step to fulfill our dreams.

LIVING WELL

For me, living well is about living in a place of peace and joy. There I can I think about what I want my life to look like, and I know that I can manifest all those desires if I stay in positive energy and push through my fears. That's the motivational model that Susan teaches and that matches my own life experiences. When I am living well, I don't question whether I am good enough or who am I to dream of a better life.

But living well as the best revenge is not about the people who have hurt you. It was never about them for me. It is about me, my health and my knowing that I do not want abuse in my relationships. Yet my own adversity has helped me champion so many women who need to assess or come out of potentially abusive relationships. As a role model for them, they might have thought that my relationship looked good from the outside. But it was plagued with domestic violence, and I was able to terminate that relationship, and that was the right thing for me to do. Today my living well allows others to see that if they have the self-determination and the courage to be triumphant, they, too, can leave an abusive relationship and move forward to find the life of their dreams.

MY THRIVER ACCOMPLISHMENTS

Moving forward with my career has been one of my major accomplishments as a thriver. I was unemployed when I first came to Susan's workshop, and through the resources she provided to me as part of her Thriver Community, I was able to work on my resume and see it as more than a piece of paper I handed to an employer in order to get a job. I remember learning that a resume presents what you have of value to an employer. Wow! I thought when I heard that. *My professional skills and education have value!* I got emotional just thinking about how much putting that label, that tag of "value," on my resume meant to me. It empowered me to get a job as a social worker and show others that I do have valuable talents and skills to give. Now I am a full-time social worker working as a clinician. I have my LMSW, and I would like to have my LCSW license in the next year.

Also as a thriver, I have been able to maintain and keep my house. There was a time after my divorce when financially I thought I might lose it, but I didn't give up, and I found the resources I needed to help me. From that experience, it became clear to me that financial stability is crucial for women who want to thrive after abuse. Last year I set up a four-session Community Action Project through my local Dress for Success affiliate entitled "Empowering Women After Abuse – Transforming Women's Financial Health Through Budgeting." Twenty- four women attended that program, and my effort drew national and international recognition from Dress for Success worldwide. That I could provide some light for these women who may have lost hope about being able to manage their finances after what they had experienced was really important to me.

A LIFE OF POWER AND PURPOSE

For me living a life of power and purpose as a thriver is an ongoing process. Although we are always evolving and changing like the butterfly, it is clear that without violence clouding our lives, we are more able to see life's purpose. I believe that God has given us all a purpose in our lives. Why we have had to experience violence is not clear, but in many cases, our purpose can grow from that experience and lift us up beyond our current circumstances. Sometimes I find having purpose in my life means just getting up in the morning to be the best I can be so I can inspire others.

I have been inspired by the women in Susan's Thriver Community who have done amazing things! One woman has become the CEO of an organization, and another has turned her land into an organic farm, a goal she accomplished after attending Susan's workshop. She connected her passion to educate people on nutrition and healthy eating to that goal, and her dream became a reality with the positive energy and support of the Susan's Thriver Community. As Maya Angelou says, "We are at our best when we inspire, encourage and connect with another human being." I believe we are hardwired as humans to connect to each other so we are not on life's journey alone. I am at my greatest when I am connected to other women and we bring forth each other's greatness.

I am a thriver! Living well is my best revenge!

— Sophia

~ ~ ~ ~ ~ ~ ~ ~ ~ ~ ~ ~ ~ ~ ~ ~

We delight in the beauty of the butterfly,
but rarely admit the changes
it has gone through to achieve that beauty.

— MAYA ANGELOU

THRIVER SUCCESS STORIES

Tawanda

*You have within you the strength, the patience
and the passion to reach for the stars, to change the world.*

— Harriet Tubman

FROM THE BEGINNING

When I first came to Susan's workshop in fall of 2016, I wasn't feeling too good about myself. I was in a very toxic, abusive relationship, and I felt trapped there without a real future ahead of me. I guess I was looking for some kind of change in my life when I met Susan. A friend of mine, my mentor, introduced me to Susan's group having attended the workshop herself previously. But in listening to her tell me the story of how the workshop changed her life, I wasn't sure I was ready for that; I wasn't sure I could do it. I did look up to her, so much so that she persuaded me to take the step and go to the workshop.

When I first walked into the room, I was excited to see other women there who were just like me. I was hearing all these good thoughts and ideas about moving from survivor to thriver and feeling the good vibes in the room, but I knew that once I left that room, I was going back into a dangerous and toxic environment in my home. It took me at least a year to really understand and utilize the *Seven Steps to Thriving After Abuse* that Susan taught me. At the same time, I had undergone the bariatric surgery that allowed me to lose over a hundred pounds. Joining the follow-up group Susan offers women after they attend one of her workshops helped me tremendously through all of this. In fact, I think that without the group, I don't think I would be where I am today. I have learned from these women – I call them my sisters – I found a sisterhood in that follow-up group. I'm just blown away by what I have accomplished in the last few years because when I walked into the workshop that day, I really didn't have any high popes. But by going through the *Seven Steps to Thriving After Abuse* with Susan and being around those positive people and their good energy, I was destined to make it. There was no way I was giving up!

THE THRIVER SISTERHOOD

Coming into the group, I was feeling like a low person, but with these women, I was a part of something bigger – my sisterhood. There, people were happy to see me, while in my regular life at that time, people weren't too happy with me. To be around people who had that good, positive energy, knowing that I could move on like them and make it in the world, felt so good. With that energy, I got the idea that maybe I could make a brighter future for myself, even though there was so much sadness with me being in the toxic relationship and struggling with so much. I dreaded going home from our follow-up gatherings. I'd stay until the last thing was cleaned up.

With all this encouragement, I began to work with Susan's *Seven Steps to Thriving After Abuse* to see if I could break through these obstacles in my life. It made sense to me that I was on a journey – victim to survivor to thriver – and I loved how the exercise for that *First Step: See Your Journey* worked for me. But I had been living in the victim role for so long, it was harder for me to do the rest of the steps at first.

THE HAPPY PERSON INSIDE

At first, the toughest one for me was *Step Three: Connect with the Happy Person Inside You.* To connect with a part of me that was happy and positive seemed impossible. As a mom with three young children and the oldest sibling in my family, I had always been counted on to take care of others and not myself. Also being in an abusive relationship at the time was destroying my self-concept, and I had sunk down into a dark place. I didn't believe I deserved to explore that Happy Person Inside, so why even bother to find out what she was about?

But I took the chance, and to my surprise there was, as Susan suggested, a part of me untouched by all that had ever happened to me. I thought I might have a Happy Person Inside, but with all the negative vibes and tension in my life, she had just gone away. Once I wrote the letter to me from the Happy Person Inside, Susan's writing prompt for Step Three, suddenly she was there! She was alive and wanted to be heard.

Here's what my Happy Person Inside wrote to me in that first workshop:

I am the Happy Person Inside and I want to tell you something...

...You have accomplished so much in your life. I am so proud of you. I want to tell you not to give up. There is greatness and great things that will come to you in the future. Remain patient. All your hard work has not gone unnoticed. Keep pressing forward, and stay with God. He will never give up on you. He has carried you thus far. You're an inspiration! Don't let your past dictate your future.

You've always dreamt of becoming a doctor, and you are well on your way. Don't let anyone or any obstacle hold you back. I will bring you plenty of business when you're ready. I know you're going to make it big. Keep smiling, honey, that beautiful smile of yours. And remember to never look back. You will never forget, but you can move forward. See those trials and tribulations as stepping-stones. I can't wait to see your name on the billboard. I'm already picking out my gown for graduation.

I love you. It's time for you to shine, honey! You deserve it!

VISION FOR THE FUTURE

After that, I also wrote in *Step Five: Vision a New Life,* a vision for the future in the voice of my newly discovered Happy Person Inside. I wrote it as if I was living that life right now. It was amazing! I had it all this there inside me just waiting to come out!

Here's what I wrote that day.

My Vision for the Future

Wow, so much is going on right now! The kids are ready. I can hear their footsteps. Oh! Look at the lights on the chandelier. They are glistening! It smells so beautiful! I did it. I'm at a banquet hall with my children, sisters, and best friend. They are finishing up with the last-minute setup. The balloons, microphones and flower assortments are all in place. My face is so clear and brown. My new business photos came out really nice. I'm celebrating the opening of my strip mall. I have an office space for my private practice, and there is also a day-care center, a hair salon, and a diner with a playscape.

Part Four

I am so psyched. I have lost a lot of weight, and I look good. I'm rocking these nice heels. I am the owner of my own businesses that I've dreamed of for some time. My sisters are all together, happy and ready to get started. I'm so overjoyed to have our home customized just how I want it. It has a huge yard that my sons keep up.

We are celebrating our family's success together without the additives (alcohol, cigarettes, and marijuana). It's so great to finally be comfortable and relax. The show is amazing! My son is singing to me while my two other kids are dancing. I'm in tears because they have accomplished their goals within the music industry. I light up when they announced my name as a "doctor." As we cut the ribbon for the grand opening of the strip mall, my kids looked over and said, "See, Mommy, now you're rich. You did it!" I reply, "We have always been rich; now we are comfortable." I owe my thanks to all the people who took time out of their lives to help me figure out mine. I appreciate and love you all.

That was the first time that I wrote about and tapped into a clear vision for my happy future life, guided by the Happy Person Inside. I was thrilled to put it all on paper! I had been dreaming about a shopping mall and what it would look like but not in as much detail. With it all laid out, I could see how it had all come to me so vividly because of my experience as a single mom with my three children over the years.

Then I was ready to work on *Step Seven: Set New Goals*. In that exercise, we write down the steps to meet our goal and we do it in reverse order. We start with the last thing we had to do to reach our goal and go down the list to the first task that would start the process. When I did that, I found that there were so many parts to my goal to create my strip mall and so many steps! But in the months since first writing them down, I found that I didn't have to focus on any one step or do them in the exact order I put them that day. I could go in whatever direction worked for me. So now I am going for it! So far, I've accomplished a lot to get to that strip mall. Recently I started working at a beauty shop, something I didn't think I would be doing right now, but the opportunity came, so I took it. So now I'm taking it step-by-step to reach my goal, and I'm not giving up!

That's one thing the women in my thriver group taught me. No matter what has happened to you, there is always hope, always a way to move through challenges and obstacles in the way of reaching your goal. But when you are in the victim state of mind, it's hard to feel that hope or feel that you can break through the hard parts. But once you get into the group and start really working on the steps, you can see how the other women are working their steps. Someone else may not have the exact same story as you, but they know the pain you feel, and when we are together, we give each other so much positive energy. I love all the positive vibes!

WHAT IS A THRIVER?

Thriving to me is about living beyond the abuse, beyond the pain. Where I am today compared to three years ago is like I'm walking on water. Now I believe that there is nothing that can stop me, except for me. I still struggle with my Inner Critic and how to keep it quiet, but that battle is nowhere near what it was before. Today, I tell myself "I want to do this" and "I can do it." There is no more "Oh, I can't" or "What's someone going to think of me?" if I do this or that. Nope! I'm going for it! I'm doing it! I shortcut all that negative chatter! I have NO time for that anymore!

How I got from survivor to thriver was to set my goals, keep my energy focused, quiet my Inner Critic and keep my vision calling to me. It feels like I'm living my fantasy in real life! It is so cool! No one else has ever done something like that before!

Now it is easy for me to go back to the thriver group and tell them where I am because the people are just so supportive of me. Susan and my sisters are so wonderful. Just being in their presences reminds me that I don't want to go backward. The only barrier to showing up as often as I could to the group was my children, being so young. But now they are older, and I can come to our gatherings and feel good. Not only am I getting something out of it, but I also know that by being there in the Thriver Zone, I'll help the "newbies" feel comfortable and open up to their Happy Person Inside too.

Recently at a workshop, I was sitting next to a woman and I wanted to move my seat because I could feel her energy and it wasn't very happy. But I had to remember that I was once that person so instead of moving my seat, I engaged with her, and she loosened up and I felt a different vibe. It reminded me that you can't judge a book by its cover, and we all need healing. We all need somebody.

Part Four

THE THRIVER COMMUNITY

Being in this Thriver Community is the best thing that has ever happened to me. I get a joy out of all of the activities, but what has been most productive for me is repeating and coming back to the two-day workshops. Even though I'm in the Thriver Zone now, there is always something I can learn. I can dig deeper and keep digging out of that victim or survivor place. I am reminded to keep going and not to push things to the side or cover them up.

Each time I go back through a workshop, I amaze myself! I start writing, and I can't stop. I write about things I didn't even know were there inside me. In some of writing journals from previous workshops, I found that there was definitely a difference in what I wrote from a workshop to another, sometimes even in the same year. There are usually similarities in what I wrote about the Happy Person Inside and my vision for the future, but sometimes I write something different in *Step One: See My Journey* and the fairy tale or children's story we write about there. But there are some awesome things that I have been saying to myself year after year as I get deeper and deeper into who the Happy Person Inside of me is, and now all that is coming out on the surface.

One of Susan's steps that I would have like to have learned earlier on my journey is how to Quiet the Inner Critic. If you hear something for so long, you start to believe it, and that's the worst feeling. It's bad enough if someone says it, but don't start believing it yourself. It will just get you down, and you'll never get back up.

LIVING WELL

"Living well" means that now I'm doing things that I thought I'd never be able to do or that I couldn't do. When I first came to the workshops, I wasn't able to get a job, and I wasn't convinced that I could get one. Going to the workshops helped me not only to quiet the Inner Critic about those doubts, but also enabled me to go through the weight loss surgery. I would never have been able to do that without knowing that I could live beyond all my challenges and have a better life.

With all the excess weight I was carrying, I couldn't stand for long. I couldn't stay awake long. Who was going to hire me? I went on interviews, and I'd fall asleep before I could be interviewed because they were taking too long to talk to me. When I did get a job, I worked at the preschool center for three hours a day, and I knew that three hours a day was not going to pay any bills. I knew that I had to do better. Today I have a better job, and I keep getting promoted to jobs with more responsibility, so I'm adding to my skills to get me to even better opportunities.

I am also doing things that I couldn't see myself doing before. Last year I took a class at the community college so I could get a certificate required for a promotion at work. I went because my Inner Critic was quiet, and I conquered my fear that I was too old to remember anything from the class. I did it, and that new certification will open doors for other positions, so I'm really excited about that.

Five years from now, I don't think I'll be at the same job. I do believe that with so many steps to accomplish yet to get to my bigger goal, I'll still be working in the human services field and looking for a location for my shopping mall space. With all the credentials I have now and ones that will be coming, I can see how doors can open up for me to many other options and possibilities.

I feel good about being in the Thriver Zone. It was difficult for me to step out of just surviving – my Comfort Zone – into the Thriver Zone. I still have some fear that I may fall back into that survivor place, but I know I can keep on thriving. I can do it! I feel very powerful at times and I have lots of purpose. I'm in the game of changing people's lives. So many people have been in my corner and helped me change mine. My way of giving back is being there to help support others and lead them in the right direction.

A LIFE OF POWER AND PURPOSE

I believe that all that has happened to me was for a purpose. The Universe has a way of teaching us lessons and preparing us for the greater outcome. I believe that if I didn't go through the things I went through, I wouldn't be here today standing strong and thriving. No matter how you were just surviving, and even if surviving felt good at that moment, once you learn that you can thrive, there is no going back. I just want to say to everyone, "Listen! Come to this side! Don't stay over there. Be a thriver! It feels so great!"

I'm happy that I can share what I have gotten from Susan's *Seven Steps to Thriving After Abuse* with other women in my life. I don't like to put too much of my story on people, but I do share it. I share the information about the Seven Steps and how Susan's workshops and the material in them helped me. I tell them that coming to a workshop is not a forced thing, but when they are ready, they should make that call or seek out Susan's books. The door is always open. I tell them, "Look at me! Look at what I have been through and how I am thriving today!" Some women look at what I'm going through right now, like with my kids, and say, "Oh my goodness, I feel for you, girl!" But I'll say, "That's nothing. You don't know what I have been through." Today, I have lost all that weight, and it feels amazing. I'm working out and getting fit.

And yet sometimes things creep back in from that victim side, and I have to shut it down. I found out recently that I'm walking on broken bones because of the abuse in my life. But when I did, I had to shut that down. Yeah, that happened! Oh well, but I'm walking now.

And when that Inner Critic starts with me and says, "Hey, remember me!" I tell it, "I know you are there, but I'm over here now, and you've got to catch up to me." I know that those negative thoughts will always come up, but I can't stay there. When you are in the Thriver Zone, you have to keep working at it. Just like you can't just come in for two sessions of a workshop or read a few chapters of Susan's book, learn about the *Seven Steps to Thriving After Abuse* and then you think you got this! You're free! No, you've got to continue to keep going through it. Work those steps and keep your eye on your goals. You can achieve them!

I'm so happy that my mentor introduced me to Susan years ago and I've met all the women in the Thriver Group. I made the call and overcame my fear.

I am a thriver! Living well is my best revenge.

– Tawanda

~ ~ ~ ~ ~ ~ ~ ~ ~ ~ ~ ~ ~ ~ ~

Take up the battle. Take it up.
This is your life. This is your world.

— MAYA ANGELOU

THRIVER SUCCESS STORIES

Tennille

You must do the thing you think you cannot do.
— Eleanor Roosevelt

FROM THE BEGINNING

When I first came to Susan's workshop, I was feeling okay about myself. I wasn't thinking that a lot was wrong in my life until Susan did the exercise with us for *Step One: See Your Journey.* She wrote "VICTIM to SURVIVOR to THRIVER" on the board and talked about how the journey after being abused was from struggle to transformation and to happy ending. It was then that I realized I wasn't living in my happy ending. In fact, I was somewhere in between victim and survivor, but I hadn't really put much thought into it.

At the time I was newly engaged and thinking, *I'm happy. This is great! I'm going to get married again.* But in the middle of the first session of the workshop, suddenly my victim mentality switched on in my brain and I thought, T*his is not right. This is not how it is supposed to feel. I wondered, Am I in another abusive relationship?* This one wasn't physical, but something was not right about it.

Then in the exercise for *Step Three: Connect with the Happy Person Inside You,* Susan had us write a letter to ourselves from our Happy Person Inside from the prompt she gave us: "I am the Happy Person Inside You and I want to tell you something." I got to thinking again – something was not right in my life. I needed to fix it. I would have to dig really deep and see what was bothering me and what was best for me. Maybe I still would marry my fiancé, but I had to figure this out.

In *Step Five: Vision a New Life,* Susan gave us an exercise where our Happy Person Inside was in the future. I wrote about seeing her running to get into shape, and she was feeling better, more energized and more positive. That made me want to go home and start running with my Happy Person Inside. Our homework assignment between the two Saturday workshop sessions was just that – do something that made us happy and write about how it felt before, during and after. So that week, I ran, and this is what I wrote about how it felt.

Running

by Tennille

I had been telling myself that I wanted to or needed to start working out again. I had been giving myself so many excuses: "You can't afford a gym membership right now," or "You'll get dizzy and pass out and embarrass yourself."

I had a lot of self-doubt, but one Sunday I said, "Self, you are going to do it." I got ready to go for a run, putting on my stretch pants, sneakers, and a hoodie. I stretched out, kind of, before I went outside, and that's when I realized I was more out of shape than I thought. I hadn't even started to run, and I was already breaking out in a sweat. Oh my God, I thought, this is going to hurt.

My daughter woke up, came into the room, and asked, "What are you doing?"

I said, "Going for a run."

"A what?" was her response.

Nevertheless, I popped my ear buds in, cranked up some Mary J. Blige music, and ran down the stairs. My heart was pounding. I opened the door, and the cold, wet fog outside smacked me in the face. I stepped briskly. I thought, As soon as I reach the bottom of the hill, I am going to go for it! Some neighbors glanced at me awkwardly, as if to say, "We never saw her dressed like that."

LOL! I didn't care!

As soon as the town cemetery came into view, I lifted one foot and then the other. I let my arms swing, and I picked up the pace. I took a deep breath and, man! Did it burn! I coughed, and my eyes filled with tears. Shake it off, I told myself, and I took even breaths instead. At this point I was halfway through the cemetery, and I wanted to look back so bad! But just to impress myself, I kept going, and I read the names on the tombstones as I ran. How ironic that I chose this route. My mind began to drift. I thought of loved ones I had lost. I said prayers for them, hoping they were resting in paradise.

Then, without even realizing it, I was running. The mixed emotions gave me a surge of energy. My breathing had become steady. I almost glanced back, but at that very moment, a big red stop sign appeared, as if to say, STOP! NO LOOKING OR GOING BACK. Keep moving forward!

I kept moving – past the cemetery, past the drugstore, past the church, and past the library, the post office, the town hall, the police department, the senior citizen center, the barber shop, and the pet store. I was whizzing by everything! Yes, I thought, you got this! The burning in my legs was bittersweet. My throat was dry, but my mind was so clear. I felt strong. I felt proud. I felt like a runner!

As I approached my complex, I slowed down. I jogged, then skipped, and finally walked. I reached my front door and looked at the device on my wrist. I had completed two miles. My heart rate was 140 bpm, and the smile on my face was priceless.

"We will be doing this again," I told myself, amazed at the confidence I had gained from my run.

So later that Sunday, I rocked a black dress with black stockings and heels (appropriate, I promise) as I reintroduced my killer calves and legs to the world!

I felt so good about running that Sunday morning, but instead of support, I got resistance from my fiancé. He asked me why I was doing this and said that he didn't really understand it. That was another "light bulb" going off in my head about the relationship. I thought that if he really loved me, he'd be like "That's great! Keep writing! Keep running!" But his response was more like, "Why are you doing this now?" He got very defensive and took it personally.

That's not very healthy, I thought. His reaction made me wonder again if maybe this relationship was not the best place for me to be. Maybe I wasn't supposed to stay. Thank goodness, I was thinking that way because I can see now that I was living in a fog when

I came into Susan's workshop. With the physical abuse in my previous relationship, the warning signs of danger were clearer to me, and so I left. But I thought this one was different. I'd been saying to myself, *"He's not hitting me, so it's really not abuse."* But accepting behaviors that were very demeaning to me and controlling – that was abuse.

I AM EMPOWERED

Suddenly something just clicked inside my head, and I felt a surge of empowerment. I knew I could keep second-guessing myself about him and our future together. I could tell myself that maybe we could get married and everything would be okay, but… "No," I said. "Snap out of it! This is abuse. It doesn't need to be physical, and I can't go through with this just to be in a marriage, to be a wife and have the benefit of being in a team." Sure, I wanted to say, "This is my husband" and "I'm his wife," but that was more about the fairy tale than the reality I was facing. I was going to settle. What if I married him and was miserable? I'd have to get divorced, and who wants to go through that? Getting out of a marriage later would be much more complicated than getting out of an engagement now.

My daughters were okay about my leaving the relationship. Somehow they knew it wasn't right too. My younger daughter was supportive; the older one just said, "Mom, I don't think he's the one for you." True, I knew he wasn't my type from the start, but he was charming and put an enchantment on me because he didn't hit me. Then too, he would cook for me and do other nice things that I hadn't had in a relationship before. But was that worth it in the long run? I knew the answer to that.

Deciding to leave him was hard, but then it got really ugly. Again there wasn't physical abuse; it was more emotional. I would come home from work, and he'd push me about when I was moving out. I told him I was leaving, but he knew that I had sold my house to move in with him. I had been thinking we'd get married and buy a new house together. So now I needed to raise money for a security deposit on a new apartment, and I had to work extra shifts at my job to do that. What did he expect me to do? I had kids, so I couldn't just go out on the street. Still I worried. *What if he does put his hands on me?* We argued a lot, and it was getting bad, very intense. I was tired. I had been working a lot. The day I finally did move out, we had a huge argument. He said at first he would help me move out, but then I guess to spite me, he told me he wouldn't. It was disturbing. I had to work through all that.

A NEW VISION

When my girls and I were out and safe in a new place, I could see that attending Susan's workshop would help me set a new vision for my life. Ending that relationship was a perfect opportunity for me to start over. I wanted to better myself and let my girls know that now it was just us. I would keep us going as we transitioned to a new apartment and a new routine.

But what was next for me? I decided I had some choices. I could join a group, volunteer, write in my journal or go back to school. I did start writing. I have about twenty thousand journals all over the place! I'd have one in the car, one on my desk at home and one in my purse so that each time something came into my mind, I would be able to jot it down and write about it. I started to volunteer, finding ways to help others, and I realized that it was time for me to go back to school. After doing some research, I started in the nursing field.

I could see that this was the right time of me to figure out who I wanted to be in this lifetime and not follow someone else's idea of that. I had gotten out of a controlling relationship where a man wanted to keep me to himself. He'd say, "You don't have to go to school. We're getting married. I'll provide for you." But to me that was a way for him to control me and not let me be my own person. I didn't see that sign initially, but now I did, and that wasn't what I wanted.

My long-term goal now is finish to my degrees and have a career in nursing. I want to have RN, then BSN (bachelor's degree in nursing) and finally be an APRN (Advanced Practice Registered Nurse). Then I'll open a wellness center using a holistic approach to getting people healthy. We'll offer yoga, essential oils and different types of therapy that will take it beyond just a medical model. That goal has now become my answer to the question Susan had us write about when we first came into the workshop: "If you had ten million dollars and all the time in the world, what would you do?" But back then I wasn't thinking that big, and I hadn't read Susan's book, *Entering the Thriver Zone,* and I hadn't met the other women in her Thriver Community. They have inspired me with their positive energy, and I know now I can do anything I put my mind to. I am a thriver!

WHAT IS A THRIVER?

Being a thriver has brought a whole different perspective to me. Before, if someone would say something or do something I didn't like, I might lash back at them because I was so hurt inside. Now I just let it go. I might focus on why they might be acting that way. Are they angry or bitter or did something happen to them to make them that act that way? I might try to talk to them and ask them what's going on or tell them that they might benefit from going to a workshop like Susan's.

But now I let the things that used to tick me off go over my head. I'm not wasting my energy on those things anymore. Of course I might get upset because I'm human, but before I was always on pins and needles, so miserable inside. Now I'm much more easy-going. Even my kids have noticed the change and say that I don't scream so much anymore. I had a lot bottled up in me – anger, resentment, bitterness, shame and embarrassment. Now I don't let anything bother me.

Thriving has allowed me to be more forgiving of myself and more compassionate even toward people who have abused me. I don't have to hug them or be their friends, but I can and do forgive them with all of my heart. Would saying that make a difference to them? I don't know, but saying it for myself makes me feel better when I'm not holding on to all that emotional baggage.

Also, letting go of negative thoughts and energy keeps me more in positive energy, something that is very important to me on my journey from survivor to thriver. I need people around me who are positive and supportive. I've gotten a lot of comfort from the classes I have taken at my church. They are free and scheduled after work in the evening so I can go and meet new people. Everyone has their own story, but we get together and share ideas, and I've met some awesome people and have made new friends.

Most of all, I've learned not to isolate myself. I did that at one point, telling myself that if I stay in the house, no one will know about this or add to my shame or guilt. But going to therapy and seeing a counselor has helped me tremendously as well as networking with others, praying, meditating and speaking my affirmations every morning to get my day kick-started.

THE THRIVER COMMUNITY

Being a part of Susan's Thriver Community has been great! No judgment is passed there, and I have connected with women who are role models for me. I can see their happiness and how talented they are with their writing or music or whatever! They are women who are not afraid to move forward with their lives, and they inspire me. If they can do it, I can do it too. I love the energy buzzing around them, and I want to be a part of it. They invite me to events or activities and give me words of support and encouragement. I love going to all our Thriver Community events where I am surrounded by all that positivity.

I wish I would have found a community of women like this sooner and been able to see signs of abuse earlier in my relationships. But I was young, and my mind was in a different place. I tried to please everyone and give them the benefit of the doubt that they'd be okay, that they would treat me with respect. Now I have more intuition, and it's great! I'll say, "I don't think that is going to work." To my younger self, I'd say "Be more alert and listen to that gut feeling you're having because it is never going steer you wrong."

I also wish I would gotten my schooling sooner. I did one semester of college after high school before I got pregnant. If I would have had a little more guidance and finished four years of college after high school, I'd probably already be an APRN. So everything in my life has been delayed, and it's harder going to school now that I'm older. But I have done much better as an adult learner, and today I'm so much clearer about what I want to accomplish and what I want my purpose in life to be.

LIVING WELL

I love when Susan tells us that living well is the best revenge. To me, living well means not hanging on to any of my bitterness. As a thriver, I've learned to process and react to things differently. Not everything needs to be argued or needs a response. Absolutely not! In fact, I'm not going to entertain thoughts like that or spend sleepless nights worrying about them. I've learned that when everything moves along smoothly, there is so much less anxiety in my life, and I can stay more focused on the important things, like living well and accomplishing my goals.

When I see how the other women in Susan's Thriver Community are living well, I can feed off of their positive energy. We bring each other up and give each other courage to move forward with our lives. I never have had to say, "Oh, that woman still looks miserable." Everyone is happy when we are together! We have a wonderful time! Susan's work has been life-changing for all of us.

MY THRIVER GOALS

Now that I am thriving and living well, my life goals are so different than when I was just surviving. I didn't think about how I wanted to help people with my nursing skills until I saw myself as a thriver. I can see today how working in the nursing field has brought up different things from my childhood. That has made me realize that I am meant to do something to help kids. Working in school nursing and then pediatrics as I have, I can see the warning signs with the kids, and certain behaviors show me that something has happened to them. I am able to help families parent their children, and that is so purposeful to me. Maybe that's because no one did that for me when I was a kid. I'm not blaming anyone, but I tell my kids, "I love you. God bless you and don't let anyone touch your body!" That little snippet is so important. No one ever told me not to let anyone touch my body, so how would I have known that? We know that kind of trauma in childhood can affect all of our future relationships.

Having my associate's degree in nursing and being in Susan's Thriver Community have helped me to move toward my long-term goal of working with women and children to help them to take their own journey beyond abuse. With my eye on having my BSN (bachelor's degree in nursing) in five years, followed by an APRN (Advanced Practice Registered Nurse), I know I can do it. My goals are attainable now.

I am a thriver! Living well is my best revenge!

– Tennille

~~~~~~~~~~~~~~~

The journey is valuable, but believing in your talents,
your abilities, and your self-worth can empower
you to walk down an even brighter path.

— SOLEDAD O'BRIEN

Discover the tools

to build your own vision.

— Mary Anne Radmacher

Part Five

LIVING IN THE THRIVER ZONE TOOLBOX

You are only as strong as the tools in your toolbox.

— MICHAEL BASTIAN

Every woman needs a toolbox! Did anyone ever tell you that in school? Probably not, but it's a necessity, particularly if you have experienced violence, abuse and trauma in your life like the women I have worked with over the last twenty years. For them, living in the Thriver Zone means being strong, resilient and, above all, practical! So that's where the toolbox come in!

What do you need in your toolbox? Some of items have already been listed, reviewed and discussed here in this book. Let's explore how one of the women who has attended my workshops described the toolbox she has created after answering the Call to Adventure on her journey to thriving beyond abuse!

THE CALL TO ADVENTURE

By Robin

The wonderful opportunity to explore my individual journey is what I call my life-long adventure. I am the hero of this adventure on which I have been able to look at and explore who I am as well as experience and learn more about my authentic self on each step of this journey of self-discovery.

It is amazing how many steps I've taken on this journey. But then there have also been missteps and stumbles as well as leaps, confident strides and persistent jogs through troubled spots and finally a stroll through happy, scenic landscapes in the latter part of my life. Along the way I have found people who, without knowing it, have been my role models. Or maybe I came away with a bit of knowledge from them, a shared experience that now I call my own.

At each step, all of these experiences have been treasures for me to add to my toolbox. Now when I open the toolbox, I see that all these exciting experiences are there for me, filling me with awareness of who I am. In my toolbox, I also find the names of people I can reach out to if I need help. I call them my friends. My toolbox holds for me too reminders of skills I have developed through trial and error. These skills are extremely valuable to me, as I can build on them and use them in the future.

I carry my toolbox wherever I go so I can focus on what is important to me. I look in my toolbox when I need to find safety, friendship and love. On each step along this journey, I find new opportunities for self-discovery, and I can take a side path, too, just to find a new, treasured experience or live in the moment and learn.

The magic of this self-discovery becomes part of my toolbox. I don't ever recall my toolbox being heavy. If anything, my toolbox feels lighter with each experience I have, and instead of feeling burdened, I seem to have grown tall and straight. Each time I open my toolbox, I am amazed at the treasures that are there. Nothing in it is useless, and I'm always excited when I can find exactly what I need each time I look for a particular skill or tool.

The breakthrough for me on this journey is that my heart has grown and I am willing to share the treasures of my toolbox. Safety, friendship, learning and love are the most treasured of the treasures in my toolbox.

Like Robin, what I hope you have gained in reading my third book in *The Thriver Zone Series*™, is how to fill up your Thriver Zone toolbox with all of the "treasures" you will need to take on your journey beyond abuse.

GATHER YOUR TREASURES

Some of these treasures you may have already collected from the life experiences you have had so far on this journey. I hope you have been able to add more from reading the stories of the seven women who are our Super Hero Thrivers in this book. They can be your role models now for how to move from experiencing the most horrific kinds of abuse, degradation and violence to surviving and even thriving! These women are strong, resilient and determined. They want their lives back, and they are moving forward every day to accomplishing that goal.

May you be like them and the hundreds of women who have come to my workshops or read one or more of my books. The motivational guidance I have successfully used with women can help you, too, if you want to do more than survive everything that has ever happened to you. You can focus on the positives, set and accomplish new goals and follow your power, passion and purpose to achieve great things in your life.

In reading this book, I hope you have also connected with the Happy Person Inside You, a part of you untouched by all that has happened, and that you continue to work to vanquish your Inner Critic's power to sabotage your journey forward. Now you see yourself as the hero of your own story and know how to answer the Call to Adventure each time, meeting new allies and friends who can help you overcome the challenges of your life and reap the reward of finding your true, authentic self – THE REAL YOU!

TAKE THE QUIZ

With all these new tools and tips from the women who are our Thriver Success Stories, I can imagine that soon you, too, will be living in the Thriver Zone and I hope will continue to do so into the future. How do you know that you are living there? What will remind you how wonderful it feels to be there? I leave you with two things at the end of this book that hopefully will answer those questions for you.

First, at the end of this Part you'll find a *Quiz: Are You Living in the Thriver Zone?* Take it now to set a base line for you to mark progress forward as start using the tools more consistently over a period of time. Then take it again and compare your answers to mark your progress into the Thriver Zone and beyond. I also left you some additional tips and tools for your journey.

Second, I give you one more wonderful piece of writing by Pamela, one of the Thriver Success Stories in this book – a Super Hero Thriver! She calls it her happily-ever-after fairy tale. Be inspired by her journey and find your own Happy Ending! We must never give up!

Finally, I love this quote by Anne Frank: *What a wonderful thought it is that some of the best days of our live haven't happened yet.* Let's believe they are there and that we can live them as thrivers!

My Happily-Ever-After Fairy Tale

by Pamela

Once upon a time in a faraway place lived a little princess who was taught that she was nothing. She tried doing only what other people wanted, but they were still not happy. She tried reading books and taking classes to be the "perfect" wonderful person, but they were still not happy. She even tried defending her ways and her children, but then each moment became unbearable and scary.

She was sure she had done something wrong. She was riddled with guilt and hated her life. Finally she reached out, and when she shared her story with someone else, she found that she wasn't alone. She started to learn that there were other ways of living and that all the negative voices in her head and from others around her were not right.

As she learned more, she questioned the Negative Nellies and began to search for her own happiness. She found joy in small moments and watched those moments grow into days and weeks of joy. One day she realized that she loved herself unconditionally and she was perfect just the way she was born. She had seen this kind of self-love in others, but finally she saw and felt it in herself.

In spite of the negative opinions that others had of her, she told herself she wasn't weird or too sensitive or even wrong. She was creative and empathic. She had good ideas, even though she didn't think and act the same as other people.

The world started to have color for her. She knew that this was only the beginning of her journey, but she was going in the right direction. She was on her way to a purposeful life – helping and loving others and creating joy one moment at a time.

She finally was living her happily ever after!

This is a journey to reclaim your life after abuse. Come take it with us, your Thriver Community! We are here for you!

Then living well is not only our best revenge, but the song of our souls and the fulfillment of all of our dreams!

—Susan

~~~~~~~~~~~~~~~

When we walk to the edge of all the light
we have and take that step into the darkness of
the unknown, we must believe that
one of two things will happen –
There will be something solid for us to stand on...
or God will teach us how to fly.

— Elizabeth Kubler-Ross

QUIZ: Are You Living in the Thriver Zone?

✎ PROMPT: Write out your answers to questions below. Review and write a few paragraphs to describe your journey to Living in the Thriver Zone. ENJOY!

1. When you first found Susan's *Thriver Zone* motivational model, how were you feeling about yourself and your future?

2. What obstacles did you have in your life to having a bright future? Did you think you could overcome those obstacles?

3. Did Susan's idea that there is a journey from victim to survivor to thriver help you?

4. What tools are most helpful to you in Susan's motivational model, including *The Seven Steps to Thriving After Abuse* and *A Road Map to Manifest a Life of Power and Purpose*?

5. What is thriver? How would you define it today?

6. Who is supporting you on this journey? Do you have role models for thriving after abuse?

7. What is one thing you thought you couldn't accomplish but you did as a thriver?

8. What do you still want to accomplish? What are your goals right now?

9. Have you been able to find a life of power and purpose as a thriver?

10. How is living well your best revenge today as a thriver?

Part 5

TIPS and TOOLS FOR YOUR JOURNEY

- Don't forget to take the *Survey for Journey to Thriving* regularly in Part Three of this book as well as the *Quiz: Are You Living in the Thriver Zone?* Measure your progress beyond your limiting beliefs about yourself and into the Thriver Zone.

- Remember the Seven Steps! Use them together or focus on the ones most helpful to you – like *Quiet the Inner Critic* and *Connect with the Happy Person Inside You.*

- Use your *Road Map to Manifest a Life of Power and Purpose* if you are working on a specific focused desire and need to overcome your fears and find the Real YOU!

- Find a group of women who support you and go through Susan's books and materials together with them by forming a *Thriver Group* of your own. (See more on how to do that on Susan's website, *www.ThriverZone.com.*)

- Set your goals and keep working at them. Never give up!

- Write often in your Thriver Zone journal or notebook that you started with this book. It is your place to write the story of your journey beyond abuse and celebrate it everyday!

- Have fun! Give yourself a break and relax. You got this!

FOR EXTRA CREDIT!

Read Susan's novels in *The Best Revenge Series*™.

Awaken: The Awakening of the Human Spirit on a Healing Journey

Emerge: The Opening of the Human Heart to the Power of Love

Inspired by a true event, these are fictional stories that capture the heart and soul of how women can thrive after abuse!

See more about all of Susan's books at the back of this book or at *www.ThriverZone.com/books.*

My Avenging Angel Workshops™ PROGRAM

SUSAN OMILIAN
Originator and Facilitator

Basic My Avenging Angel Workshops™ – The two six-hour sessions, based on the idea that living well is the best revenge," are conducted by Susan Omilian for women who have been abused. With writing, focusing and interactive exercises, the sessions help women take the journey from victim to survivor to thriver. Connecting to the thriver energy inside them, they can push through their fears and set new goals so they can reclaim their lives and move permanently out of the cycle of violence.

The Archangel Follow-up (Advanced) Group is a community of the women who have taken both sessions of the basic workshop and meet regularly for support, guidance and encouragement from Susan and each other so they can stay connected with their thriver energy. Activities include monthly follow-up sessions to share a pot-luck lunch, check in on their short- and long-term goals and engage in writing and creativity exercises as well as hear guest speakers on topics such as finances, health and wellness. Other positive, upbeat activities include summer events and a seasonal holiday party.

The Stepping Forward Program – Experiencing abuse can derail a woman's dreams, curtail her education and limit her access to good jobs. Some women are financially strapped due to lack of control of money during the abusive relationship and lengthy legal battles with abusive ex-partners. The Stepping Forward Program is an economic empowerment effort for women who have attended the basic workshop to focus their career goals, sharpen job skills, build their own businesses and manage finances so that they can move forward in life without severe economic and financial consequences.

Journey to the Real You Weekend Retreats – The annual Archangel retreat is a time to reflect, reenergize and renew the commitment to move permanently out of the cycle of violence. Set at a retreat center in a beach house on the shoreline, the three-day retreat allows women to unwind in a beautiful setting and, through writing, interactive exercises, music and dance, connect again with the "Real You," a part of them untouched by all that has happened to them.

In conducting her workshops and follow-up activities since 2001, Susan has developed a motivational model for women to take the journey from victim to survivor to thriver. The model is included in The Thriver Zone Series™ of books and materials.

Susan can provide My Avenging Angel Workshops™ in your area. In Connecticut, they are provided free of charge with costs for weekend retreat underwritten by a scholarship fund.

Contact Susan at Susan@ThriverZone.com or through her website www.ThriverZone.com

Part 5

SPEAKER/TRAINER PACKET
for ENTERING THE THRIVE ZONE
with Susan M. Omilian JD
Award-winning Advocate, Author, Motivational Speaker

In the early morning hours of October 18, 1999, Susan received a phone call that her nineteen-year-old niece Maggie had been shot and killed by her ex-boyfriend on a college campus in Michigan. Maggie was brilliant and beautiful, an athlete and a musician whose dream was to go to law school and help others. At the moment of her death, Maggie didn't have the chance to survive so Susan vowed to work with women helping them not only to survive but to thrive after abuse as Maggie could not.

In Maggie's memory, Susan has originated and facilitated since 2001 her *My Avenging Angel Workshops*™ based on the idea that *living well is the best revenge.* Described as "life changing" and "a component for women recovering from abuse that has been virtually overlooked," Susan's work has helped hundreds of women break the cycle of violence and live happy, productive lives after abuse.

Susan is the author of several books that contain the motivational guidance she has successfully used in her workshops. With simple easy-to-read work sheets, invigorating writing exercises and inspirational success stories, these books help women take the critical "next-step" beyond surviving to reclaim their lives after domestic violence, sexual assault and child abuse and live well as a thriver.

Susan is an experienced keynote speaker, workshop facilitator and trainer who has presented her work nationally and internationally to victim advocates, service providers and survivors and their families. She can speak on these and other topics.

- **ENTERING THE THRIVER ZONE: Living Beyond Abuse in Our Lives**

    When Susan's niece was killed in 1999, a victim of dating violence, Susan transformed the tragedy into a unique opportunity to help others move beyond the abuse and trauma in their lives. Susan now empowers women with a motivational model she has successfully used in her *My Avenging Angel Workshops*™ and contained in her books, including *Entering the Thriver Zone: A Seven-Step Guide to Thriving After Abuse.* In her presentation, Susan demonstrates the writing exercises and worksheets she has used with hundreds of women guiding them on the journey from victim to survivor to thriver! As a survivor, victim advocate or provider, you'll be inspired by Susan's award-wining work and see how women can live well as their best revenge.

    In half- and full-day presentations, Susan demonstrates her motivational model and shares the compelling real-life stories of women she has mentored who are thriving today after abuse.

- **TELLING MAGGIE'S STORY: Exploding the Myths about Dating Violence**

    Maggie was a smart, strong-willed young woman who knew how to take care of herself. How could she become a victim of dating violence? In telling the story of her nineteen-year-old niece killed by an ex-boyfriend, Susan explodes the myths about dating violence and illustrates the warning signs of abuse in a relationship. Her talk can audiences see Maggie's tragic death as a cautionary tale and a call to action to end violence against women.

    Appropriate for students (middle school to college), parent groups and general public.

Contact Susan at *Susan@ThriverZone.com.* Visit *www.ThriverZone.com* to view her *Thriver* video.

RESOURCES

CRISIS INTERVENTION

For immediate crisis intervention services in your local community, contact:

- The National Domestic Violence Hotline 1-800-799-SAFE (7233) **www.thehotline.org**

- National Sexual Assault Hotline at 1-800-656-HOPE (4673) **www.rainn.org**

- National Center for Victims of Crime **www.victimsofcrime.org/help-for-crime-victims**

- Office for Victims of Crime, U.S. Department of Justice. **www.ovc.gov**

DATING VIOLENCE AND STALKING

- Break the Cycle: Empowering Youth to End Dating Violence **www.breakthecycle.org**

- Love Is Respect – National Teen Dating Abuse Help Line 1-866-331-9474 **www.loveisrespect.org**

- End Stalking in America **www.esia.net** provides information and assistance to potential victims and those currently being harassed, including a list of state laws against stalking.

- The Sanctuary for Victims of Stalking **www.stalkingvictims.com** offers sanctuary and resources on stalking to victims, how to identify stalking and deal with it through online support groups.

- Women's Law.org **www.womenslaw.org** is a project of the National Network to End Domestic Violence, providing legal information and support to victims of domestic violence, stalking, and sexual assault.

DOMESTIC VIOLENCE

- National Network to End Domestic Violence (NNEDV) **www.nnedv.org** offers support to victims of domestic violence who are escaping abusive relationships and empowers survivors to build new lives.

- National Coalition Against Domestic Violence (NCADV) **www.ncadv.org** works closely with battered women's advocates around the country to identify the issues and develop a legislative agenda.

- **www.domesticshelters.org** Free, online, searchable database of domestic violence shelter programs nationally.

- National Resource Center on Domestic Violence (NRCDV) **www.nrcdv.org** is a source of information for those wanting to educate themselves and help others on the many issues related to domestic violence.

SEXUAL ASSAULT

- RAINN — Rape Abuse & Incest National Network www.rainn.org operates the National Sexual Assault Hotline and has programs to prevent sexual assault, help Victims, and ensure they receive justice.

- National Sexual Violence Resource Center **www.nsvrc.org** provides leadership in preventing and responding to sexual violence through creating resources and promoting research.

- The Victim Rights Law Center **www.victimrights.org** is dedicated solely to serving the legal needs of sexual assault victims. It provides training, technical assistance, and in some cases, free legal assistance in civil cases to sexual assault victims in certain parts of the country.

CHILD ABUSE

- Childhelp USA National Child Abuse **www.childhelp.org** directly serves abused and neglected children through the National Child Abuse Hotline, 1-800-4-A-CHILD® and other programs.

POST TRAUMATIC STRESS

See information listed at National Institute of Mental Health website, **www.nimh.nih.gov**.

Resources

BOOKS ON JOURNALING AND CREATIVE WRITING

One to One: Self-Understanding through Journal Writing and Life's Companion: Journal Writing as a Spiritual Quest by Christina Baldwin

The Artist's Way: A Spiritual Path to Higher Creativity by Julia Cameron

Journal to the Self: Twenty-Two Paths to Personal Growth by Kathleen Adams

Writing Down the Bones by Natalie Goldberg

Bird by Bird by Anne Lamont

BOOKS ON PERSONAL GROWTH AND SPIRITUAL DEVELOPMENT

Secrets about Life Every Woman Should Know: Ten Principles for Total Emotional and Spiritual Fulfillment by Barbara De Angelis

Anam Cara: A Book of Celtic Wisdom by John O'Donohue

The Seven Spiritual Laws of Success: A Practical Guide to the Fulfillment of Your Dreams by Deepak Chopra. Also, *The Path to Love and How to Know God*

Care of the Soul and Soul Mates by Thomas Moore

A Return to Love and A Woman's Worth by Marianne Williamson

Something More: Excavating Your Authentic Self and Simple Abundance by Sarah Ban Breathnach

You Can Heal Your Life by Louise L. Hay

Sacred Contracts: Awakening Your Divine Potential by Caroline Myss

Faith in the Valley: Lessons for Women Who Are on the Journey to Peace by Iyanla VanZant

The Gifts of Imperfection: Let Go of Who You Think You're Supposed to Be and Embrace Who You Are by Brene Brown. Also, view her TED Talks at **www.TED.com**

Wherever You Go, There You Are: Mindfulness Meditation in Everyday Life by Jon Kabat-Zinn

BOOKS AND WEBSITES TO EDUCATE AND INSPIRE YOU

It Could Happen to Anyone: Why Battered Women Stay by Alyce LaViolette and Ola Barnett **www.alycelaviolette.com**

Why Does He Do That? Inside the Minds of Angry and Controlling Men and Daily Wisdom for Why Does He Do That? by Lundy Bancroft. For other books, visit **www.lundybancroft.com.**

Macho Paradox: Why Some Men Hurt Women and How All Men Can Help by Jackson Katz **www.jacksonkatz.com**

Trauma and Recovery: The Aftermath of Violence from Domestic Abuse to Political Terror by Judith Herman, MD

Beyond Trauma: A Healing Journey for Women by Stephanie S. Covington, PhD **www.stephaniecovington.com**

I Closed My Eyes: Revelations of a Battered Woman by Michele Weldon **www.micheleweldon.com**

The Verbally Abusive Relationship and Verbal Abuse Survivors Speak Out; On Relationship and Recovery by Patricia Evans **www.patriciaevans.com. www.verbalabuse.com**

From Ex-Wife to Exceptional Life™: A Woman's Journey through Divorce by Donna Ferber **www.donnaferber.com**

Miss America by Day: Lessons Learned from Ultimate Betrayals and Unconditional Love by Marilyn Van Debur **www.missamericabyday.com**

A Thousand Splendid Suns by Khaled Husseini, author of *The Kite Runner*

Coercive Control: How Men Entrap Women in Personal Life by Evan Stark

Scared Silent: A Memoir by Mildred Muhammad **www.mildredmuhammad.com**

Invisible Chains: Overcoming Coercive Control in Your Intimate Relationship by Lisa Aronson

Becoming by Michelle Obama

Daring Greatly: How the Courage to Be Vulnerable Transforms the Way We Live, Love, Parent and Lead by Brene Brown See also her subsequent books at **www.brenebrown.com.**

The Hero with a Thousand Faces by Joseph Campbell and other book

MOVIES TO ACCOMPANY YOU ON YOUR JOURNEY

Miss Americana (2020). In this documentary, Taylor Swift, singer/songwriter, shows incredible courage on her journey from the muzzled "nice" girl to a woman with a voice. She deconstructs her entire belief system about herself and finds true power in her voice, musically, politically and emotionally. She is a thriver!

Little Women (2019) The classic Louisa Mae Alcott story about four sisters growing up during the Civil War is reimagined in modern era to show their strength and courage despite adversity.

Bombshell (2019) In the #MeToo era, a workplace story of sexual abuse told from the victims' point of view showing how their empowerment incited a movement that reverberated worldwide.

Wonder Woman (2017) A woman raised as an Amazon warrior, leaves home to fight a war and in the end, discovers her full powers and true purpose in life.

Beauty and the Beast (2017) – Belle is more empowered in this movie version. She likes to read and learn and doesn't want to marry a hyper-masculine man.

Cinderella (2015) – A newer version with Lily James of Downton Abbey. Best line, "I forgive you!"

Wild (2014) with Reese Wetherspoon – True story of Cheryl Strayed, who undertook a 100-mile solo hike as a way to recover from her mother's untimely death.

Saving Mr. Banks (2013) – The woman who created the Mary Poppins stories takes on Walt Disney.

Philomena (2013) with Judi Dench – Inspiring journey of unmarried mother to uncover truth about the son she was forced to give up decades earlier.

Frozen (2013) – A story of an epic journey to help a sister and put an end to her icy spell.

Sleeping with the Enemy (1991) with Julia Roberts – An abused woman gets a life!

Eat, Pray, Love (2010) with Julia Roberts – A woman's quest to rediscover and reconnect with her true, inner self.

Enchanted (2007) with Amy Adams – The ultimate "real-life" fairy tale with a big production number in Central Park, New York City.

Enough (2002) with Jennifer Lopez – An abused woman fights back.

Shallow Hal (2001) with Gwyneth Paltrow and Jack Black – Beauty lies within.

Riding in Cars with Boys (2001) with Drew Barrymore – Based on a true story of a woman's life.

Paying It Forward (2000) with Helen Hunt – No good deed goes unrewarded.

Billy Elliot (2000) – A young boy finds his dream in ballet despite his father's disapproval.

Erin Brockovich (2000) with Julia Roberts – A woman who doesn't give up and helps others!

Ever After (Cinderella) (1998) with Drew Barrymore – The best happy ending.

How Stella Got Her Groove Back (1998) – Stella takes inventory of her life.

Titanic (1997) – Rose lives on to find the life of her dreams.

Waiting to Exhale (1995) with Whitney Houston – Be happy with who you are.

The Color Purple (1995) with Oprah Winfrey – Based on Alice Walker's novel.

Muriel's Wedding (1995) with Toni Colette – The hapless Muriel finds herself!

What's Love Got to Do With It (1993) – The triumph of Tina Turner.

A League of Their Own (1992) with Madonna and Rosie O'Donnell – A sports story for women!

Enchanted April (1991) – Rent a villa in Italy and see what happens.

Thelma and Louise (1991) with Susan Sarandon – Girls rock even as they careen in a car over a cliff.

Fried Green Tomatoes (1991) – Based on Fanny Flagg's novel about the Whistle Stop Café.

Cry for Help: The Tracy Thurman Story (1989) – A true story about overcoming injustice and achieving social change.

The Burning Bed (1984), starring Farrah Fawcett – Still a riveting story.

MUSIC TO SOOTHE YOU

Michael Hoppe: *The Yearning – Romances for Alto Flute (with Tim Wheater)*

The Unforgetting Heart, Solace and *The Poet – Romance for Cello*

Raphael: *Music to Disappear Into I and II*

Movie Soundtracks: *Possession and Secret Garden*

Enya: including *A Day Without Rain* and *Paint the Sky with Stars*

David Lanz: including *Cristofori's Dream*

Loreena McKennitt: including *The Book of Secrets*

Thank you for reading the third book
in Susan M. Omilian's *Thriver Zone Series*™

Living in the Thriver Zone

A Celebration of Living Well as the Best Revenge

Also Available – Susan's first two books

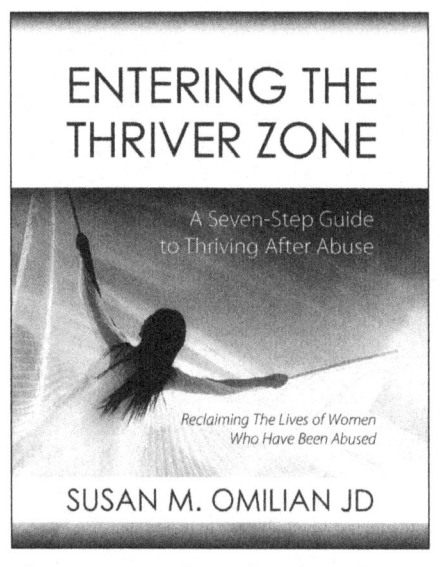

Entering the Thriver Zone

A Seven-Step Guide to
Thriving After Abuse

Staying the Thriver Zone

A Road Map to Manifesting
Your Power and Purpose

Connect with Susan about her books and her work with women at
www.ThriverZone.com

Susan's books are available nationally on Amazon.com, BarnesandNoble.com
and locally at your library or favorite bookstore.

For autographed copies, order on Susan's website, www.ThriverZone.com.

Contact Susan (Susan@ThriverZone.com)
for bulk purchases at quantity discounts.

Now Available
Susan's first two books in *The Best Revenge Series*™

*A story inspired by true events that captures
the heart and soul of how women can thrive after abuse.*

Awaken

The Awakening of the
Human Spirit on a
Healing Journey

Emerge

The Opening of the
Human Heart to
the Power of Love

Coming NEXT in *The Best Revenge Series*™

Thrive

The Journey of the Human Soul
to Discover a Life of Purpose

Connect with Susan about her books and her work with women
www.ThriverZone.com
www.facebook.com/ThriverZone
www.twitter.com/ThriverZone
www.pinterest.com/susanomilian/Thriver-Zone
www.linkedin.com/in/susanomilian
www.youtube.com/susanom1